C000176649

LOOKING FORWARD – LOOKING BACK

ALSO BY DULCIE GRAY

Murder on the Stairs
Murder in Melbourne
Baby Face
Epitaph for a Dead Actor
Murder on a Saturday
Murder in Mind
The Devil Wore Scarlet
No Quarter for a Star
The Murder of Love
Died in the Red
Murder on Honeymoon
For Richer, For Richer
Deadly Lampshade
Understudy to Murder
Dead Give Away
Ride on a Tiger
Stage Door Fright
Dark Calypso
The Glanville Women
Anna Starr
Mirror Image

For children
Death in Denims

Non-fiction
Butterflies on my Mind
The Actor and his World
   (with Michael Denison)

Looking Forward –
Looking Back

an autobiography

Dulcie Gray

Hodder & Stoughton
LONDON SYDNEY AUCKLAND TORONTO

British Library Cataloguing in Publication Data

Gray, Dulcie, 1920–
   Looking forward, looking back.
   1. Acting. Gray, Dulcie, 1920–
   I. Title
   792.028092

   ISBN 0-340-52080-9

Copyright © Dulcie Gray 1991

First published in Great Britain 1991

All rights reserved. No part of this publication may be
reproduced or transmitted in any form or by any means,
electronic or mechanical, including photocopying,
recording, or any information storage and retrieval system,
without either prior permission in writing from the
publisher or a licence permitting restricted copying.
In the United Kingdom such licences are issued by the
Copyright Licensing Agency, 33–34 Alfred Place,
London WC1E 7DP. The right of Dulcie Gray to
be identified as the author of this work has been asserted
by her in accordance with the Copyright, Designs and
Patents Act 1988.

Published by Hodder and Stoughton,
a division of Hodder and Stoughton Ltd,
Mill Road, Dunton Green, Sevenoaks, Kent TN13 2YA
Editorial Office: 47 Bedford Square, London WC1B 3DP

Photoset by Rowland Phototypesetting Ltd,
Bury St Edmunds, Suffolk

Printed in Great Britain by St Edmundsbury Press Ltd,
Bury St Edmunds, Suffolk

To Michael, with love always

Acknowledgments

I would like to thank Margaret Body for editing this book, and for making the process greatly enjoyable, Mrs Edith Upton for typing the first draft and Miss Valerie M. Campling the final one; also Eileen Leahy, who, after running our houses in London for over twenty years, still helps us in a crisis, and still cares for all our dogs.

As with all my books, Michael read and commented constructively on the first draft – a nerve-racking business for both of us, but the marriage survives!

Photographic Credits

The author and publisher are grateful to the following for some of the photographs reproduced in the book:

Zoe Dominic for *A Coat of Varnish* (facing p 176).
The late Angus McBean for *Love Affair* (facing p 113), *Let Them Eat Cake* (facing p 129) and *Where Angels Fear to Tread* (facing p 144).
The John Vickers Archive for the picture Michael took to war (facing p 65) and *Brighton Rock* (facing p 80).

1

Sitting next to Somerset Maugham at a luncheon one day in the 'fifties, at the house of Lady Headfort, the famous ex-Gaiety Girl, I asked him if he had felt no guilt at using the real lives of the young men and women he had met in Malaya in such detail that they were easily recognisable. In particular I asked him about the heroine of his play *The Letter* who had shot her lover six times, and whose great-nephew and niece I had taught in the jungle when I was sixteen.

'You hurt a great many people,' I said.

Maugham, looking like a bull frog with his mottled leathery skin, turned down mouth and squat body, replied, 'My dear Mrs Denison, art is more important than life.'

I was too much in awe of him to make a reply.

If I am ever going to write down how life and art have used me, now seems the time to do it.

I have been married to Michael Denison for over fifty years and have enjoyed it enormously.

The wedding was in April 1939 and just over a week later, on May 8th, I started on the stage as a professional actress. We also started our joint career on that date, playing Simon and Sorel in Noël Coward's *Hay Fever*, at His Majesty's Theatre, Aberdeen. Stewart Granger was our leading man, and his first wife Elspeth March was our leading lady. I remember that first night vividly, and the smell of the floor polish in that clean and lovely theatre is still strong in my nose.

I can also remember Kuala Lumpur as a country town, and Walling-ford (then in Berkshire, now in Oxfordshire) with 4,000 inhabitants, and a working flour mill in the High Street. Women wore hats and gloves to go out of the house. Little middle-class girls in private schools wore liberty bodices and straw hats with streamers in the summer – summers that were so hot that sunstroke was not unknown. Men raised their hats to women, opened doors for them, offered them their seats in buses and trains and stood when they came into a room.

As a child I caught tiddlers in the Thames with a little white net and put them in jam jars. Children could play all day in the fields and woods, with no fear of rape or abduction. I collected birds' eggs (I shudder at the thought now), and butterflies (worse) and treacled for moths (horrible). I also collected live snails and let them loose in the school cloakroom because I loved the multicoloured trails they left behind them. Poppies stained the yellow cornfields with scarlet, and when the corn was reaped it was made into stooks which looked like tiny wigwams.

My mother and father were married in 1910 at St Mary Abbot's Church, Kensington. In a contemporary newspaper cutting, he was described as 'Mr Arnold Savage Bailey, Solicitor, London, and Advocate and Solicitor of the Straits Settlements, youngest son of the late Mr Alfred Bailey, Barrister-at-Law, and grandson of the late Mr Edward Savage Bailey, President of the Incorporated Law Society', and she as 'Miss Kate Edith Clulow Gray, youngest daughter of the late Mr Samuel Gray, Solicitor, and granddaughter of the late John Clulow, Solicitor to the War Office' – a plethora of lawyers! She wore a 'gown of ivory crêpe-de-chine and a court train of ivory moiré lined with chiffon, caught at the waist and shoulders with true lover's knots'. Her veil was 'lent by Mrs Burt' whoever she may have been, and it covered a wreath of white heather. There were eight bridesmaids wearing 'dresses of ivory satin and large black crinoline hats, wreathed in purple heather and coloured tulle'. Miss Kathleen Clulow Gray, described as my mother's 'niece', was the train bearer, which comes as a surprise to the present generation of our family, as none of us has ever heard of her.

My mother and father had their honeymoon in Cornwall and set sail for Malaya where they lived until their deaths.

Not long ago I was given a silver dressing-table set which belonged to my great-grandmother, and was told that she and my great-grandfather, Mr Edward Savage Bailey (President of the Law Society), spent their whole marriage in a ménage à trois with a 'foreign Count'. There were seventeen children (my grandmother was the eldest) and when Edward died, her lover (?), his lover (?) gave her the set inscribed with her name – Ellen. Were some of the children his? All of them? And how in Edward's position in Victoria's reign was such a thing tolerated in society?

By the time I was born my father had his own firm, Bannon and

Bailey, and had left Singapore to live in the Ampang Road in Kuala Lumpur.

I was the youngest child and, until I was taken back to England to go to boarding school, I didn't meet my brother and sister. They had already been sent 'home' to stay with our Bailey grandmother as Malaya's heat and humidity were considered bad for European children. My actual birthplace I am told was the Police Officers' Mess in Venning Road, Kuala Lumpur and the time midnight. Perhaps my parents were at a dance there. What an inconvenience for them if so! But then my birth must have been an inconvenience anyway, as Michael met a woman soon after we were married who was astounded that I was alive and well, because my mother was so reluctant to have me that she was high diving almost until the day of my arrival.

In an interview for one of the tabloid newspapers lately, I described my mother as unmaternal, and this was translated into unloving, which was not true. I am quite certain that she loved me dearly; in fact the certainty that I had her affection gave me security throughout the years of my childhood without her, and still gives me an inner optimism.

When she was quite young her mother divorced her father and married a rich Dutchman called Van Lorn. It was sensational to have a divorce in the family in those days. Somewhere in her childhood she learned not only to become an excellent horsewoman, but how to crack a stock whip, throw a lariat and whistle more beautifully than anyone I have ever heard. She was mad on amateur theatricals. Later she studied painting under the great Tonks at the Slade, wearing bloomers and her long chestnut hair down to her waist. (Augustus John was briefly enamoured.) She was extremely clever and spoke several languages fluently.

She had a lovely and distinctive handwriting and indeed quite exquisite hands. Later in life she wore a monocle, lace ruffles at the throat and wrists of silk dresses she often made for herself, and special mannish felt hats from Lock's. She told us that she was the third Girl Guide – Sir Robert Baden-Powell's sister was the first, a Mrs Jansen-Potts the second and my mother the third. When Sir Robert married, his wife became the first and my mother was demoted. She 'left the movement'.

My father was small, precise, conventional and always beautifully dressed. The attraction of opposites, it seems. Compton Mackenzie recognised me as my father's daughter sixty years after they had been to school together at St Paul's, although I was introduced as Dulcie Gray. 'The same tiny eyes. The same wide smile,' he said. I never had the feeling that my father had much affection for me, but my mother certainly loved him. Every morning as he left for the office, she gave him a buttonhole of the violets she had grown specially for him.

I remember very little about my first few years in Malaya. I had a half-Indian nanny called Nanny Ghouse whom I met again years later when I was acting in Kuala Lumpur for the British Council. Every morning she used to take me to the large grass lawn called the 'padang' to play with the other white children in front of the Tudor-style Selangor Club called the Spotted Dog. Every morning I demanded to kiss 'itou black Uncle' which was a darkish green marble bust of Edward VII standing on a plinth outside the rose-coloured, exuberantly ornate Federal Buildings – the Malayan Parliament. I remember being a bridesmaid dressed in a white chiffon dress embroidered with 'pearls' which had a cross-over bodice, and I wore a sort of white doily on my head, also edged with 'pearls'. I fought the page for my fair share of the train, and the bride's dog tried to join in. I went as a rose-bud to a children's fancy dress party, and for some while was so ill that I was expected to die, although I remember nothing of this last at all.

When I was three and a half, my parents took me to England on a Japanese ship. Ironically, in view of what was to happen to her, my mother loved everything Japanese and for some odd reason detested the Chinese. The journey took three weeks. I don't remember my father on the trip, only the Japanese captain and crew, an English bully boy, and my mother.

The first meeting with my brother and sister didn't go quite as planned. To my great excitement, an operation had been performed on a passenger during the voyage and while my siblings were away for a few moments I cut open Roger's golliwog, stuffed it with grass, and then had no means of sewing it up. A fierce fight ensued.

Little Gran, as Granny Bailey was called, was tiny. She wore a lace cap and carried a silver-topped cane. She was very interested in Froebel education and her daughter Dorothy – Auntie D – had been trained as a Froebel teacher. She ran a school at my grandmother's house, 79 Onslow Road, Richmond, Surrey, and was never allowed to marry, as being the only girl with six brothers she was supposed to look after Granny, and Granny lived until she was eighty-four. Auntie

D also had tiny eyes and a wide smile! And a round pretty face.

It was summer in England and our reunited family went down to Cooden for a holiday with Mummy's brother, his wife and our two girl cousins. The older children caught butterflies from a buddleia bush and put them into 'stink bottles'. Seeing their beautiful wings flapping more and more feebly until they died made me feel ill with horror, and a passionate love for British butterflies was born.

2

I suppose my father came with my mother to leave me at St Anthony's, the kindergarten in Wallingford where I was to spend the next eight years, but if so once again I was unaware. It was a bitterly cold day and I remember it as snowing. Perhaps I went to school late that term, as it certainly wouldn't have been snowing in September. It must have been cold though, because I was dressed in a white fur coat and hat and long grey gaiters to just above my knee. I had a white fur muff on a cord round my neck, and carried a small silver knife and fork, which I still have. The furs I never saw again.

The school stood in the middle of Wallingford High Street; a pleasant whitewashed, three-storeyed Georgian house with green shutters and a green front door. My mother told me to ring the bell while she paid the cab, but I couldn't reach it. It was the only time I was to use that entrance. All pupils went in by a side door which led down a passage into a courtyard between the main building and a pretty little redbrick house. At the far end of a redbrick garden path was another charming old redbrick house with a green dovecot which housed a pair of white doves. Flower-beds flanked the path. I remember a very old yew tree with a bench in front of it, and a walled gravelled play area.

In those eight years I only stayed in private houses with families for a total of fifteen weeks. The other holidays I spent with the school. Except of course when my parents were back.

Oddly enough several children like me, with parents abroad, went on the stage when they grew up: Vivien Leigh, Margot Fonteyn and Angela Thorne, for instance. Was it because we had had to learn how to become especially adaptable and independent and that being so often with strangers had given us an exaggerated wish to please? In my own case I gained popularity by clowning, so I clowned my head off. It is a talent that has been under-used as far as my career is concerned. My childhood also gave me a lifelong diffidence.

It was an excellent school, and I was reading *Treasure Island, The*

[14]

Water Babies, The Wind in the Willows and *The Cloister and the Hearth*
by the time I was six. My favourite book though, and one that I kept
in my knickers most days, was a mawkish tale called *Misunderstood*,
about a little boy misunderstood by his adored parents. I kept other
books and food in my knickers, too, because I was often sent to bed
for talking too much and liked to be prepared. It made walking
normally very difficult!

Miss Violet Hedges, the headmistress of St Anthony's, was a friend
of Auntie D. She wore mauvish stockinette knickers with elastic round
the knee, which sometimes showed. She was fair-minded and kind,
and much loved by us all. We called her Auntie. Nearly all the teachers
who came and went had long hair, either in a bun or plaited in
'earphones' over their ears, and nearly all of them had had their
fiancés killed in the Great War, except for a Mrs Glover who had
short hair, was very beautiful and had been a governess to royalty in
Siam (like Anna Leonowens in *The King and I*). She later ran a hat
shop in Sloane Street.

I was quite happy at the school, and as far as I know was never
homesick. Perhaps at four years old one doesn't miss home as much
as when one is older. Perhaps on the whole I was phlegmatic, in spite
of sudden flurries of temper. I was, however, aware of a feeling of
imprisonment, and night after night I used to get out of bed to raid
the larder for currants to take out with me on fine nights into the
garden, to sit under the yew tree or wander up the path in the
moonlight. I needed this sense of freedom, and fantasised about
beggars and tramps and escaping over the roof tops.

Apart from two rather disastrous holidays in England with my
parents, the two houses I visited for holidays couldn't have been less
alike.

At Christmas I spent one week a year with my father's eldest brother,
Cyril Bailey. He was a classical scholar at Balliol, still remembered for
'Bailey's Lucretius'. He was Oxford's Public Orator for many years
and numbered Harold Macmillan and Edward Heath among his
pupils. He, too, had tiny blue eyes and a wide smile. He was gentle
and civilised. At a party given by Fleur Cowles at Albany, Macmillan
(or Lord Stockton as he had become that day) insisted on me sitting
beside him.

'Tell me what we have in common,' he said.

I racked my brain.

'My Uncle Cyril Bailey taught you Classics,' I said.

'Ah!' he replied affectionately, 'he was the sweetest man I ever met.'

We got on well after that. On my uncle's retirement from Oxford, Edward Heath was head of a delegation from Balliol to find out what the students could give him as a farewell present. They discovered that there was no indoor lavatory at the new house he was moving to in East Hanney, so they suggested that they should give him one. My uncle demurred at being remembered (and remembering Balliol) by a lavatory, so they gave him gravel for the garden instead.

His wife, Aunt Gemma, was a daughter of Mandell Creighton, the famous Bishop of London who wrote five excellent volumes of the *History of the Papacy* and was amusingly pilloried by Lytton Strachey in his book *Portraits in Miniature* (1931). She was beautiful but always dressed in a blazer and low-heeled shoes and she was nearly stone deaf. Walking along the High in Oxford as a very shy little girl, I suffered agonies, screaming the answers to probing questions about God and the Universe, but I loved her very dearly.

Mrs Mandell Creighton was still alive at this time. As a young woman, she too had been a great beauty. In old age she looked like an enormous black tent, and she seemed to dislike children very much. She had a Grace and Favour apartment at Hampton Court where I visited her once or twice. Soon after our arrival, her spinster companion would lead all the children who had come to lunch, to the Hampton Court maze, and there leave us literally to get lost. Hot, tired and hysterical we were collected when the meal was ready, and washed and tidied and ushered in to eat.

Mrs Creighton was a friend of Bernard Shaw's and of Beatrice and Sidney Webb, and she used to chair some of their meetings.

In the South of France in the middle 'sixties, I met a formidable woman who preferred men to women. Her daughter-in-law said, 'She will address only about two sentences to you, but don't be frightened of her. She means no harm.'

Nervously I waited for my two sentences.

'I hear you are an actress, Mrs Denison,' she said.

'Yes.'

'What have you been acting in?'

'*Candida*,' I replied.

'Bernard Shaw's *Candida*?'

'Yes.'

'In London?'

'Yes.'

'He was a friend of mine,' she said. 'I often went to his meetings. Sometimes there was a woman on the platform called Mrs Mandell Creighton. She was always dressed in black and wore big black boots. I was terrified of her.'

'She was my aunt's mother,' I said.

'Good heavens!' she exclaimed anxiously, and from then on she seemed actually nervous of me!

Another story about this woman delights me. When she was handing over her French estate to her son, he told her that he wished to have the chapel rededicated, and that he would like her to come to the service.

'Of course I won't!' she said. 'What an idea! You know quite well that I have been an atheist all my life.'

'I want you to come, Mother,' he insisted. 'All the staff will be there, and many of my friends.'

She went. She wore an enormous hat and sailed up the aisle to the front pew.

During the course of the service, the clergyman said, as he had said thousands of times before: 'Thou didst not abhor the Virgin's womb.'

She drew herself up to her full height in outrage.

'I did not come here to listen to pornography,' she said, and left the chapel.

Aunt Gemma and Uncle Cyril were passionate socialists. They had four children, Mary, John, Rachel and Susan, and they lived in a bitterly cold house called The King's Mound. There was a nursery with a rocking horse and Cousin John had a toy theatre in cardboard with cut-out figures, which I adored. The nursery was ruled by a small brown-haired vigorous woman called Baa, and if she was in the kitchen one could communicate with her by a tube, with a cork which one unplugged then whistled down and talked into. The kitchen passage had a mass of little iron bells with curly handles fixed on wires, and a panel which indicated which room was ringing which bell. There was always a black labrador dog who monopolised the fire in the living-room, but the fires in all the rooms seemed woefully inadequate to a child from Kuala Lumpur. All the family were wonderfully kind to me, and made me very welcome.

The other house I visited belonged to the parents of my great friend at St Anthony's, Jane Boulenger, who spent almost as long as I did at the school. Jane had a merry face with brown eyes, scarlet cheeks and light brown hair. She was a chic child with a good brain and a great sense of humour. We are still friends, but in those days we had an intense rivalry as well as our friendship. One day I told Mrs Boulenger fiercely, 'Jane saw a swan's nest today, but I saw a mare's nest.'

I paid the Boulengers three visits. Jane's father was E. G. Boulenger, an outstanding zoologist who created the reptile house and the aquarium at the London Zoo. He was a great practical joker and I found him very entertaining but a little frightening. His wife had trained as a dressmaker and while still in her teens joined a Sloane Street theatrical costumiers, and designed the costumes for the original *Peter Pan*. On the first night, Barrie asked her to be part of the claque to start the applause when Peter asks for the audience to help save Tinkerbell's life. It wasn't needed then, nor ever has been since.

Peter Pan in their company was the first play I ever saw. I didn't enjoy it. To begin with I hated Mr Darling infinitely more than Captain Hook. Mr Darling was rude to the dog Nana – and that was enough for me. By the time the crocodile appeared with the clock in its stomach, my nerves were at breaking point, and I was transferred from Mr Boulenger's lap to the theatre Wardrobe, where for the rest of the performance I taught the wretched wardrobe mistress how to one two three hop.

Laurence Olivier was very frightened on his first visit to the theatre, too. He was taken as a little boy by his mother, and they sat in the stalls. There were two sets of curtains on the stage. The blue brocade ones parted to reveal red velvet ones. As these, too, began to rise, he shivered in nervous excitement. His mother took his hand. 'Don't be frightened, Larry,' she said. Larry recalled that ever afterwards in the terror of his own first nights he remembered this, and wished his mother had been there.

The Boulengers shared a house in St Mark's Square, Regent's Park with Dr Vevers who was the Zoo doctor, and on Sundays Jane and I were allowed 'backstage' to see the new arrivals or the sick animals, to hug the chimpanzees and feel the snakes, which to my surprise had dry, not slimy skins.

Another colleague of Mr Boulenger, Joan Proctor, had painted the scenery for the snakes' cages. She kept a chimpanzee called Johnnie whom she used to bring to the Boulengers for tea. (Was he the fore-runner of the chimpanzees' tea party at the Zoo?) When Johnnie was coming Mr Boulenger used to blow up a balloon, paint a face on it, put a hat on it, then tie it to a coat hanger over which a jacket was hung. This 'scarecrow' was then arranged in a chair. Johnnie would chatter with excitement when he saw it, but before he was allowed to play with it, he had to sit at the table with a bib tied round his neck and have his tea, which consisted of a banana. When he was allowed to get down, he circled the room making little clicking noises and getting closer and closer to the 'balloon man'. At last he reached it and, with extreme caution, he jabbed at it with his index finger and leapt back as it exploded. He seemed to love the joke.

Joan Proctor also kept a cat and a snake and all three spent the night on her bed. Sadly, when she went on a long visit to America, Johnnie died of a broken heart.

My other holidays were spent, with other children whose parents were abroad, at the staff houses of other schools. We wore uniforms except on Sundays. Most of these holidays were enjoyable. One was a nightmare. There were only four of us that time, my sister Rosamund, who had come to St Anthony's for a year, and two others, and we went to stay with the school matron, a highly emotional woman with a small dark moustache, who read Dickens to us in the evening, which we loved. It was the first time I was aware of that most beautiful of English sounds, a blackbird singing in a may tree. We collected birds' eggs and there was great rivalry. The local farmer said that if we found a plover's nest, only the one who had discovered it first was to be allowed the egg. I found the nest but Matron gave the egg to Rosamund. I was upset and outrageously rude – so rude that I was locked in the bathroom all night alone with Matron's uncertain tempered brindle bull terrier bitch. I spent the night in the empty bath and every time I raised my head the bull terrier snarled at me. I used the experience later in one of my horror stories.

One thing I was aware of was that in these institutionalised years I missed someone to whom I knew that I was special. It was sometimes difficult to be so self-sufficient – to pass my exams well, to be top in dancing or drawing, in fact to sustain a wish to achieve – only for my own satisfaction. While it was a good schooling for independence of mind, it had an element of boredom which I recognised even as a child. Early on I had had a literal belief that God was watching me, and that comforted me. I had been taught that God was everywhere and had been shown pictures of him as an old man with a long white beard, dressed in long white robes. I looked for him enthusiastically but fruitlessly.

He never appeared until one day we walked in a crocodile across the fields to the church at Mongewell because our vicar in Wallingford was on holiday. This church had the very high old-fashioned pews that one never sees nowadays, which at my height entirely cut me off from seeing anything but the roof. The time for the sermon came and I was sitting unexpectantly fairly near the front when suddenly the Reverend Hughes mounted the pulpit steps – an old man with a long white beard, dressed in a long white robe. Wild with excitement, I leapt to my feet on the pew.

'Hurray!' I shouted triumphantly to an astounded clergy and congregation. 'Hurray! There's God!'

I was told that God could never be seen and, disappointed, I dismissed him as my much needed audience.

I suppose a child's character is formed by the time he or she is eight years old. Mine was already split down the middle as my later life has shown. I was an introvert and extrovert (writing and acting), fond of companionship and fiercely independent (marriage and a career), placid and passionate, observant, detached, and even then determined to appear to be as other people wanted me to be; but I had already achieved one thing, I could be on my own and never feel alone. This is a piece of luck.

The world that enveloped my childhood was a slower, gentler, more solitary world than the present one, free of pollution in the sea, air and on land, and much less populated by humans. I look back on it with pleasure, as I live now with pleasure, but it is with pleasure mixed with apprehension that I look forward to the future.

Humans are conquering nature. Is it a solitary battle, or a war that is being won? Has nature any trick up her sleeve? I hope so.

3

I was a plain child, and one of the most popular games we played at school was Weddings. Though almost never chosen as the bride, I was nearly always a bridesmaid – perhaps because of my successful clowning. On one exciting day, however, I *was* actually chosen as the bride, and we were just about to start the game when I was told to go and get tidy because my mother was in Auntie's drawing-room.

My mother!

Every week she had sent me a letter in her beautiful handwriting. She had also sent me extraordinary and original presents, some books from her childhood, and an exquisite model Chinese town in porcelain with houses and bridges and pagodas and ponds, and little men in long robes with beards and Chinese caps on, and little women with intricate headdresses and robes and tiny bound feet. She also sent cardboard cut-outs of Chinese men and women with clothes made of real silks and satins and their beards and hair made of real hair. My beloved godfather, Uncle Jum, my father's favourite brother (who was physician-in-ordinary to King George V, and had campaigned successfully for the blind to become physiotherapists, and for radiology to be accepted in this country), had once sent me a doll sitting in a cart pulled along by a clockwork ostrich complete with feathers, but my mother's presents were always the best. Now here she was in person and I had entirely forgotten what she looked like, although I had longed for her every day.

I have no idea what I expected but certainly not what I saw. Both my mother and I gave each other a great shock. She was now fat, with her red hair piled on her head in plaits, and she sported a monocle. My first words were 'Hello Mummy, I was married this morning.'

My parents stayed in England for several months that time. In the summer they rented a cottage at Cranham, a small village in Gloucestershire. It came with a cook and I suppose a cleaner. There were a great number of beams in the cottage, and the ceilings were very low. My father continually banged his head on them. He did his best not to swear in front of us, and usually exclaimed 'Oh my ker-um-pet. My crumpet!' which I thought hilariously funny. There was quite a large garden with a few fruit trees and a double outside lavatory in a shed, where two people could sit comfortably side by side on wooden seats, and fuller's earth was provided to throw down the chute.

My mother, remembering her days as the third Girl Guide, made us get up at six in the morning to gather firewood so that we could make fires in small brick kilns on the lawn. These we had to light with only three matches, to bake potatoes by hanging them on a hook over the fire. This took most of the day. She also whistled divinely to the birds and gave us a bantam each. My bantam cock liked roosting on the clothes line in the kitchen at night. The other two slept in a coop-and-run in the garden, and were eaten by foxes.

My father was as keen as my mother on amateur acting and they got up a show in the village hall. (Frustrated actors often have professional actors as children, so my fate was coming nearer but I didn't know it!) I was to be a part of the show. They were to sing 'Yes, we have no bananas' and I was to rush to the stage from the audience with a bunch of bananas, shouting 'Yes, you have'. Unfortunately I fell asleep and never got there. I don't remember being chastised for this or indeed for anything else by my mother. A dog called, I think, Nipper, who had been left behind when its owners went on holiday, adopted us, especially my mother. Sometimes she drove us stylishly around in a large dark blue Overland tourer which she called The Blue Lady. Daddy never learned to drive. Neither have I.

At Christmas we went again as a family to a place called Damerham in Norfolk. As presents my sister and I were given grey wolf fur coats and muffs, and I painted a Christmas card for my parents of a robin, which enchanted my mother who decided that I should follow in her footsteps as a painter.

My parents went back to Malaya after Christmas and their next two leaves taken at two-yearly intervals were spent in Switzerland because my father was now an asthmatic and mountains were supposed to be a cure. He must have been doing very well at this time because the Hotel Belvedere et Grande at Davos, and the Vereiner Hotel at Klosters were first class and extremely expensive, but strangely we children were never given any skiing lessons, though my mother did lend me to two young Americans she didn't know as ballast for their boblet. Sonja Henie used to skate for our pleasure on the ice-rink at the Belvedere and my mother, who sewed beautifully, made me frocks and told us all wonderful stories in the evening when we were dressed and ready for the hotel dinner. We would choose the titles – 'The Elephant and the Ant' for instance – and she always found a way of including both.

There was a fancy dress ball that Christmas, and she went as Joan of Arc in armour made by herself out of cardboard painted silver, with gold staple pins for the rivets, and she won first prize. The hotel hairdresser came most evenings to wave my very straight hair, which I hated. I used to brush out the waves after dinner with a damp hairbrush. I was also a favourite with the professional dancer at the hotel, and we often had to do an impromptu exhibition dance together, which was very popular as I was ten and small and he was in his forties and a tall man. This I also hated. Boarding school doesn't fit one for showing off!

My mother considered me very lucky and would send me downstairs with a ten centime piece to get 'more change' from the slot machines. I was expected to bring back a jackpot.

I remember two things in particular from this holiday. From time to time I have told lies. Everyone has, and since I grew up I have lied constantly about my age, because casting directors are strangely rigid on this topic, but I have never been able to lie without guilt since one dinner time in Davos when I refused to eat my pudding when I was told to.

'Why not?' demanded my mother, exasperated after several refusals.

I thought wildly.

'Because I've got measles,' I said triumphantly.

'My God!' exclaimed my mother. She rushed me from the table, up in the elevator to my room where she threw me into a hot bath, then looked behind my ears. There were spots. I *had* measles! I've never been more astonished! In fact there had been an outbreak in the hotel, of which I suppose I had been vaguely aware.

The other occasion I recall was weird. My mother was always very popular with the young married set and, before dinner, several of them used to visit us for drinks. One couple was a Scandinavian Beauty Queen married to an obsessively jealous American. The following year, back in Malaya, my parents received a Christmas card from them. It had been drawn by the husband. It was a bizarre caricature of the wife with one of their children clinging to the Statue of Liberty, and the husband with the other child clinging to the Eiffel

Tower. All round this central picture were medallions showing past, present and future scenes. In one medallion was a picture of the husband pointing a gun at his wife. Shortly afterwards the wife shot and killed her husband, and her plea of self-defence was accepted by a French court. The most telling piece of evidence for the defence was the Christmas card.

When I was eleven I left St Anthony's for a school in Wokingham. Auntie took me there herself in her bull-nosed Morris Oxford. This had to be cranked by hand, it ran out of water and when it rained I hopped out from time to time to wipe the windscreen with sliced raw potatoes. I was only there a year but it was my first chance to do some acting and I made a small sensation as one of the princes in the Tower. I was cast for Sir Andrew Aguecheek as well but tore a ligament before the performance.

My holidays changed too. I now went to a holiday home in Norfolk with my brother Roger. While staying there we were allowed to go to the theatre in Norwich where we saw *The Ghost Train, Hit the Deck* and George Robey. With *Peter Pan* and *Babes in the Wood*, these constituted my entire theatrical experience before I went to drama school. But we saw films, among them *The Three Monkeyteers* acted entirely by monkeys, *Dr Fu Manchu*, and the first talkie, *The Singing Fool*.

Our last holiday with our parents was at Instow in North Devon, but by then our family fortunes had taken a nose dive. My father had invested disastrously in rubber. His firm was still going though, and he was an 'unofficial member' of the Malayan Federal Council elected to represent the coloured races, for which later he was to receive the CBE. During these holidays they were invited to a Buckingham Palace Garden Party but otherwise the going was hard. They quarrelled a good deal, especially over my mother's unpaid bills, and the Marine Hotel at Instow was small and simple. We sailed, and watched my father play cricket. Embarrassingly he nearly always got a duck, although as a young man he had played very well, and he was a member of the MCC, I Zingari, the Free Foresters and the Devon Dumplings. I was allowed to go to the village dances, and Mummy got up a tremendous Wild West Show for the church, which included nearly everyone in the village, made a lot of money, and ruined the vicar's lawn. At Instow I saw Yvonne Arnaud, who was on holiday. She was pointed out with awe.

Before they set sail for Malaya, taking Rosamund with them, my

[24]

parents saw me confirmed wearing a sort of white evening dress which my mother had unfortunately found for me. Roger and I were left behind, I for a final school term and holiday, Roger for another whole year.

By some oversight, the arrangements for my last holidays were very vague. A family in Instow called Paul were meant to take me on a motoring tour through Europe for some weeks, but it was discovered that I was always car-sick, so they went without me. Instead I shared a cottage with another friend of my parents called Joanie Preston-White. She was one of a variety of eccentrics who lived in Instow in those days. She knitted socks for another eccentric called Lord Charles Kennedy, who was some years ahead of the fashion as he liked to have every toe differentiated – 'like gloves on his feet', Joanie used to say. In or out of these socks, he was attractive to women and one summer evening the district nurse, crazed for love of him, stripped and turned cartwheels on the lawn. She was taken away by the village policeman. In order to pay my fare to get to London to the aunt and uncle who were to be my last hosts before I too left for Malaya, I sold a friend my lacrosse stick.

My uncle and aunt then took charge of me, and I went on a shopping spree to Berwick Market where, off the rails, I bought a pale blue satin evening dress with a jacket with white fur cuffs, a bathing costume (a one-piece Jantzen) and a long-sleeved brown crêpe dress. Except for the bathing dress, nothing was exactly tailor-made for the tropics and a shade temperature of 80° Fahrenheit, but I loved my grown-up evening dress because grown up from now on I determined to be.

4

My mother's arrangements for this voyage were far from vague. I was to travel with Lady Caldecott. Olive was the charming but over-sensitive wife of Andrew Caldecott, the Chief Secretary of the Federated Malay States. He was later to become Governor of Hong Kong and was a brilliant and amusing man, as full of practical jokes as Mr Boulenger. He sometimes played the organ in St Mary's Church, Kuala Lumpur, improvising on tunes like 'Stop Your Tickling Jock' for the voluntaries. He had also composed the state anthems for some of the Malay Sultans for their various regal appearances under their ceremonial umbrellas. Some of these tunes were excruciatingly funny. I now find this a little alarming.

Olive was sea-sick on day one, so I was commandeered by Lady Clementi, the wife of the governor of Singapore, who took me under her formidable wing. She looked like a Burne-Jones model, with masses of fair golden-red hair, large eyes, a short pretty nose and excellent skin. She had a high authoritative voice and was very kind.

The journey took roughly three weeks and life on board, even for a fourteen-and-a-half-year-old with very few clothes, was extremely social. Men far outnumbered the women, and even I had an admirer, a young Chinese who had been to Oxford where he had suffered no racism, but was now being ostracised for the first time in his very rich life. I was up dancing every night and so was Lady Clementi who danced the waltz to everything the band played.

The ship was completely full, its cargo containing quantities of livestock which were freshly killed for the various gargantuan meals eaten every day in the first-class dining-room: a four-course breakfast, a six-course luncheon, a large tea served from four until five o'clock, and a seven-course dinner. The second-class passengers fared only slightly less well. Mahatma Gandhi was on board travelling second-class, and his legs were so thin they looked like cocktail sticks.

Fresh supplies of animals, poultry, vegetables and fruit were taken on board at every port for of course there were no freezers. Evening dress was worn every evening (my new evening dress came in very handy, both with its jacket and without! So did my confirmation dress), and to my amazement I was never sea-sick.

At Gibraltar Lady Clementi showed me the baboons, whose survival is superstitiously linked with a continued British presence on the Rock. At Marseille she took me to see the Château d'If where the Count of Monte Cristo was supposed to have been imprisoned, but she mistook the way back to our ship and I was very puzzled by my cabin which had none of my clothes in it, although in every other respect it was identical. I rang for the steward who was unfamiliar too, and discovered that we were on the P & O sister ship, called I think the *Strathnaver*, which was about to sail for England.

At Port Said the gully-gully men, in red fezzes and soiled white cotton robes, came on board to make pathetic looking little day-old chicks appear out of what seemed thin air, and performed brilliant sleights of hand with scruffy half-starved rabbits and coloured paper streamers. Snake charmers playing high-pitched dirges on flutes to swaying cobras also invaded the ship. Ashore the men went to Simon Arszt to buy new topees; a great excitement for the young men going out East for the first time.

As the great ship steamed down the Suez Canal escorted by a busy little pilot boat, I saw the first of many dramatically brilliant sunrises and sunsets. In the mornings the Eastern sky turned yellow, the colour intensifying in one spot which rapidly deepened into a vivid carmine, spread itself quickly over a vast area, streaked with bands of threatening grey, paled to pink and faded. Suddenly the sun, already hot and blazing yellow, wheeled above the horizon and, flashing in glory, sailed into the azure sky.

In Aden tiny Arab boys dived over the steep sides of the ship to collect the pennies and sixpences the passengers threw for them, and caught them in their mouths under water. We visited the bazaars in Colombo, then went up into the cool of the hills at Kandy.

At Penang my father and mother came on board to meet me, with Amin our head boy, a handsome Javanese in his late twenties. My Chinese boyfriend came to say goodbye, but my mother froze him off, and we travelled to Kuala Lumpur on the night express (the 'kerater sombong' as the Malays called it), the proud car. At dinner on the train we ate an excellent curry waited on by smart Indians in scarlet and white uniforms, and we had lace-covered bunks with clean sheets to sleep in.

Kuala Lumpur railway station is turreted and honey-coloured, designed a hundred years ago by a Scottish engineer and still one of my favourite buildings in the world. Betjeman would have loved it, too.

My sister Rosamund was waiting for us at home on the Kia Peng Road, also the entire staff consisting of a kebun (a Malay gardener), two syces (Malay drivers), a Chinese cook, a second boy, and a tukan ayer (water carrier and general dog's body). There were also two ayahs, the elder one who acted as my mother's lady's maid, and 'Little Ayah' who looked after Rosamund and me. My mother's ayah would have been pretty but, in common with most Malays, she chewed betel-nut which reddened and discoloured her teeth. 'Little Ayah', a child of thirteen or so and therefore marriageable, was ravishing. The Malays are a beautiful race.

The extent of my parents' financial trouble soon became clear to me although they still seemed to live in some luxury. This was why I had been taken away from school and why, sadly for my mother's ambitions for me, I had not been sent to an art school to study painting.

The house was a whitewashed bungalow, built Malay fashion on stilts, and it had an arched porch. (It has been pulled down since and the Belgian Embassy stands in its place on the corner of the race course.) It had a large and attractive garden with a badminton court in it. Inside the house the rattan furniture, with holes in the arms of the chairs for the drinks glasses, was painted black, and there were brightly coloured cushions, many of them orange. The curtains were chintz. The big living-room was on two levels; the entrance part on the lower level, leading through a beaded curtain to the dining-room, and two shallow steps, left and right, led up to the sitting areas. There were two ceiling fans which whirled steadily, and a bedroom and dressing-room on either side at the ends of the bungalow, which opended on to verandahs. My 'room' was the left-hand verandah.

That all was not well in personal relationships was also immediately evident, and Rosamund had had a very bad time. Mummy and Daddy were quarrelling almost daily, and Daddy adored Rosamund which had aroused my mother's jealousy. My mother also disliked the fact that when the telephone rang, it was nearly always for Rosamund, who was beautiful and had many boyfriends.

Malaya at this time was of course part of the British Empire, although not as a result of conquest. The British connection had come about in an almost haphazard way. From the establishment of East

India Company trading posts in Penang and Port Moresby in the eighteenth century, and the founding of Singapore (thanks to the genius of Sir Stamford Raffles who recognised the strategic importance of this almost uninhabited island consisting chiefly of mangrove swamp) and Malacca in the 1820s, there had followed a gradual development of spheres of influence in the larger native states. Their population, and indeed their rulers, saw the advantages of living under the security of the British rule of law, rather than in the primitive chaos enlivened by Chinese pirates and Siamese marauders to which they had become accustomed. From this unlikely material there had evolved a Government in Singapore with important outposts in Kuala Lumpur and Penang in which the Chinese (the majority), the Malays, the Indians and the British, lived together with a remarkable degree of tolerance, if not enthusiasm for each other's cultures. The Malay Sultans kept their state, but the British Royal Family was everyone's Royal Family and, since the situation had come about through enlightened self-interest on everyone's part, it seemed to work until the fall of Singapore in 1942. Self-interest is a great spur to achievement. The British Indian empire came about because at a crucial moment the Dutch put up the price of peppercorns.

Our days followed a fairly rigid pattern. Rosamund and I had to get up at 6 a.m. to clear the enormous snails off the leaves of the cannas, which they ate. The snails had been brought to Malaya by a snail lover some thirty years previously and during that time had developed into monsters the size of golf balls. We were supposed to drop them into ayer busok (or disinfectant) in pails, where they rapidly dissolved into bubbles. I hated this and threw them over the hedge on to the race course, where during the race meetings, the horses sometimes sounded as if they were running on cobble stones.

This chore over, we had early morning tea and fruit (mangoes, mangosteens, pawpaws, chicous and ramboutans), then we bathed, dressed and went to the dining-room for a full cooked breakfast with bacon and eggs, fish, kedgeree, kidneys, prawns in batter, and toast and marmalade. In mid morning there was often a mah-jongg party of Mummy's friends, with tea and biscuits and chocolates. Just before lunch we had sherry, gin slings or stengahs (whisky and soda), with an occasional treat of sherry cobblers, a very complicated cocktail at which my mother was an expert – with machan ketchils (little eats). Tiffin (lunch) consisted of soup, fish, meat (or on Sundays a Malay curry – our curry tiffins were famous), pudding, cheese and fruit. As the temperature was a constant 80° Fahrenheit, this was quite a luncheon. We had tea and fruit at four o'clock and twice a week we had guests over to play badminton. At six o'clock there were more drinks and more machan ketchils. Dinner at eight was a full Edwardian meal.

Rosamund and I played a good deal of tennis, swam at the Lake Club pool in the Lake Gardens, one of the loveliest parks in the world, went to race meetings and dances, for which owing to the lack of European girls we were often booked up for months ahead. Even I had a regular boyfriend, who had seen me at the Kuala Lumpur railway station and had written me a passionate letter ending 'hasta la vista', which I thought very dashing.

We sometimes went shopping in the morning. The various races all wore their own national costumes. The Malay women were in fitted jackets of voile or lawn with coloured sarongs, the Chinese in big white shirts and black trousers with sandals, or brilliant satin cheong-sams, and the Indians in pale muslin saris, often shot with gold thread. Although there were many Japanese, they kept a low profile until the war.

We had two dogs, a rough and a smooth-haired fox terrier. Binkie the rough-haired one, and my mother's adored companion, loved killing snakes. Jane the smooth-haired one loved raising them from their resting places under the stilts of the bungalow. Jane would find them and bark them out into the open. Binkie then rushed in, caught them behind their heads and shook them quickly to death. My father had been responsible for bringing in an anti-rabies law which decreed that every dog should have an injection. To show the way, although Binkie had already had one, he was forced by my father's own law to have another and it killed him. Jane missed him terribly and was soon put down.

My mother had an extraordinary dislike for the Chinese. I have no idea why. In the afternoon while she was resting, she was often disturbed by Chinese barang men. She told Amin to get rid of these itinerant vendors and both sides became angrier and angrier as the barang men persisted in coming. Finally the Chinese waged a sort of war against her and instead of coming once a week they came every day. Mummy and Amin became frightened, until Mummy remembered that Cookie was Chinese and asked him to put up a notice board at the bottom of the drive telling the barang men to keep out. He did so and Sir Cecil Clementi (the Governor and a noted

Chinese scholar), arriving to play badminton one day, was horrified at what he saw. He demanded that Mummy should take the board down, describing the message as 'unutterable filth'. As he visited us about once a year, and the barang men now came daily, the notice board stayed where it was.

If there had been no tensions at home, it would have been a wonderful life, but violent tensions there were.

Daddy was away all day, either at the office or at the Parliament buildings, so it was the evenings when we were all at home that were the dangerous times.

If my parents were in a good mood, they played 'I've gotta motta' from *The Arcadians*, a show they had seen and enjoyed in London. To help play the records which buckled in the heat, they used Flit to stick the needle in the undulations. If they were in a bad mood, they played 'The Ride of the Valkyries', which as a prelude to a row is a piece of music that can't be bettered. I still can't hear it without a beating heart.

Daddy's asthma was now very bad and his only relief came from smoking Potter's asthma cure which sparked and crackled in his pipe. He needed injections every night and his arms and back were pitted with marks.

Rosamund left home to become a schoolmistress at the jungle station of Fraser's Hill. Roger left school in England to come to Malaya to pass his law exams to go into my father's firm, and I was sent for two terms to St Mary's, Kuala Lumpur, as the only European girl. As a minority of one, I was treated with great kindness and consideration.

It was virtually the only time that I was on equal terms with the other races in Malaya, something I much regret now and regretted then. I made especial friends with a Chinese girl, the daughter of Sir Chu Kia Peng, and went with her to her magnificent home in Kuala Lumpur, where in the main room there was a huge painting of Sir Chu in morning dress with a top hat. I wasn't allowed into the domestic quarters, but owing to my mother's dislike of her race, my friend wasn't allowed to come to my home at all. A beautiful Indian girl called Jaya was another friend, but before I could become properly integrated I was removed from St Mary's to join Roger who was having a bad time with a crammer – a beachcomber smelling of whisky, with a dirty white tutup (Chinese style) jacket, with whom neither of us learned anything.

We moved at about this time to a pleasant two-storeyed house, also in Kuala Lumpur (perhaps it was cheaper), but life at home was becoming impossible for me. The rows were undiminished. I used to give Daddy his evening injections and he drank too much whisky and became maudlin and tried to maul me about. It was horrible and intolerable and I resented it forcefully. There were threats that I should be banished to a convent on the grounds of disobedience (!) and I was given other dark warnings. I found that I couldn't concentrate on my exams, and the ceiling fans went on whirling monotonously. My mother used to go to bed directly after dinner so that more often than not I had to spend the rest of the evening alone with my father which I detested, until I too could escape to my room and shut myself in.

Things came to a head on Armistice Day. My mother and father left me locked in my room with Little Ayah to keep me company, when they went to put a wreath on the cenotaph. I told Little Ayah to pack a suitcase for me, and called for the kebun to put a ladder up to my window and then get hold of a rickshaw. Little Ayah and I slid the suitcase down the ladder and I climbed down after it with Little Ayah in floods of tears begging me to be sure I married the 'fattest man in the world'. (If he was fat he was bound to be rich.) The rickshaw arrived, I ran away for good and it was the end of my childhood.

5

If I have made my father out to be a monster, it is because that is how he seemed to me at that age, but of course he wasn't. His chronic asthma was exhausting, especially in such a hot climate, and he was a man under extreme stress. The great success he had made by hard work was crumbling about his ears, and he was trying to put a good face on his near bankruptcy. He needed comfort and wasn't getting it. In one's teens one tends not to appreciate the problems of grown-ups. They are the adversaries, the enemies of one's own eager life force. My mother too must have been having a very difficult time. She loved him and she loved me. At this point Sir Cecil Clementi offered my father a probationary judgeship.

The legal system in Malaya was different from that in England, being closer to Lord Mackay's proposed reforms of 1989. In the press cutting of my father's wedding, he had been described as 'Solicitor, London, and Advocate and Solicitor of the Straits Settlements'. In Malaya at that time, as there were no barristers as such, the judges were appointed from other colonies. This meant that they were not in the least conversant with the languages and customs of the country in which they were to practise. Sir Cecil found this absurd. Daddy had a good reputation and, to Sir Cecil, his appointment made sense, but first my father had to leave his own firm and that was a wrench. He also found it difficult to find a successor of whom he approved, and to whom he wished to sell, although he needed the money so badly. Finally he arranged matters and was posted to Johore.

When I ran away, I went to Raymond and Gwen Madge. Gwen had been the librarian in Kuala Lumpur and she already knew and sympathised with my dilemma. I stayed with her while I sat for my School Certificate at St Mary's. I passed and, through my mother, was accepted as an assistant schoolmistress at St Margaret's, Fraser's Hill, for five shillings a week and board and lodging; so in September I joined my sister. I saw my mother many many times after I had run away, but she never once referred to it. Neither did I.

[33]

Fraser's Hill is still my Shangri-la and, until six years ago at least, it had hardly changed. I am told there is now a high-rise hotel and chalet-type bungalows. It is sixty-three miles from Kuala Lumpur and is reached by a road running first north through rubber plantations and then at a small town called Rawang turning east and climbing up through the jungle by a narrowing valley towards the mountains. At the Gap the real climb begins, on a fiercely twisting gated road reserved for upward traffic at odd hours, and downward traffic at even.

The jungle, too, is my favourite milieu. Its profusion lifts the heart. Vast trees, some of them supported at their base by trunks wider than thirty men standing with linked arms, carry other trees on their top branches, also of considerable size. From many of them, cylindrical strands – up to six inches wide and often more than 150 feet in length – plunge into the earth below, as stout as ships' masts. Beneath these giants flourish coconut palms, Nipa palms (which produce the betel-nut), great tree ferns, bamboos and smaller, vividly flowering trees. Under these again there are ground orchids, lesser ferns and aromatic shrubs. The earth is red round Fraser's Hill. Rattan creeps along the ground or climbs the tree branches, knotting them together with strands hundreds of feet in length. Monkey cups, insect-eating pitcher plants and multicoloured flowers make a bright forest carpet. At the very tops of the tallest trees, scarlet and orange flowers, seldom seen, blaze at the sky and liana cascades from branch to branch bearing huge clusters of orange blossoms. The animals keep out of sight during the day and, until nightfall, only a king cobra or a panther would attack humans unprovoked, or a man-eating tiger, ill and hungry and too slow on its feet to catch a faster prey.

There are hornbills and toucans, brain fever birds and bantam fowl and, at night, the argus pheasant. There are huge, harmless jungle tortoises with green shells and red bodies that hiss like snakes to protect themselves. There are enormous butterflies the size of a small bird with vast wing spans, which glide in the jungle groves. There are delicious noises both day and night – crickets, the musical two-toned bell-sounds of tree frogs, and the beetle chorus dominated by the coconut beetle whose call accelerates up the scale in height and intensity, then stops and starts again. These calls are often answered by the disapproving clicks of chik-chaks, which defy gravity indoors on walls and ceilings and are transparent, so that you can see their little bodies filling up with the flies they catch as food.

In the early morning, wah-wah monkeys leap from branch to branch out of the thick mist below the tops of the trees, the females clutching their young as they spring, making strange liquid cries.

St Margaret's was a low whitewashed bungalow with a red corrugated iron roof. (Six years ago when I revisited it, the roof had been painted green but almost nothing else had changed.) It was ugly to look at and ordinary, but it was set in paradise. There was a small garden round it with a low wall and then, immediately, the jungle. From one part of the garden there was a wonderful view over the tree tops to the mountains – pale blue in the distance.

Inside it had a central passage with rooms off it on either side, except at the far end where a large room filled the width of the building. The large room doubled as a large classroom and as the staff sitting-room at night. At the other end was the dining-room and the headmistress's office. There were twenty-six pupils aged from four to fourteen and a half, mostly boarders and, when I first went there, a staff of three – the headmistress, Rosamund and me.

The work was moderately heavy. The tiny children had to be dressed in the morning and, between breakfast and prayers (Rosamund played them into prayers and played the hymns), they had to be potted. This, if the children aren't your own loved ones, is not a chore to be recommended. Prayers were at nine. Lessons were from nine thirty until lunch time, with a short break at eleven for milk and biscuits on the small lawn. After lunch there were organised games on the 'padang' a few hundred yards away and, after tea-time there was prep. Then the small children had to be bathed and bedded. The larger children in due course to be settled down – exercise books to be corrected, and finally leisure.

In our free time, we played golf on the little nine-hole golf course at the bottom of our jungle path, and on Saturday nights there was an informal dance at the Selangor Club beyond the padang. The weather was like a South of France summer and, as Fraser's Hill was a holiday centre with bungalows for the various British firms that operated in Malaya, there were always plenty of young men on call. I was very happy there.

In due course Rosamund moved to a bigger school at Cameron Highlands, and St Margaret's was bought by a splendid Scotswoman with the shoulders of a stevedore, the smile of an alligator and several warts on her ugly face, who bought me (I was after all very cheap) with it. She was one of the bravest and kindest women I have ever known. Her adored husband, her childhood sweetheart, had died after a grim struggle with cancer, leaving her penniless. Within weeks she had borrowed money and bought St Margaret's.

Rosamund and I had two fascinating holidays together; the first in Johore Bahru where, among other things, we saw our father pronouncing the death sentence in his first case, and hating it, and where we attended the coronation of the Sultan's first European wife. He was in his sixties, she in her thirties and it was her second marriage. She had been Mrs Green, the Scottish wife of the local doctor. She had fair hair, splay teeth and for the coronation wore a white hat with a brim which came down to within inches of those teeth. I have noticed that women with splay teeth always get their man. She had two passions which, ultimately, led to her downfall. She loved dancing Scottish reels with alarming energy emitting Scottish yelps, and she loved playing bridge in the morning. The Sultan put a veto on the yelps and the bridge. When he discovered her at a morning bridge party after the veto, he dragged her out of the room by her hair, saying 'I divorce you. I divorce you. I divorce you.' As he was a Muslim, that was that.

On the other holiday, we went to stay with one of Rosamund's boyfriends, John, who was a District Officer in Pahang. He was probably in his late twenties and very attractive. In common with many young men out there, he was responsible for an area roughly the size of Wales and, like most of the others, he did an excellent job and was honest, just, and well respected. Many of them lived alone, miles from anywhere, often with a fiancée waiting for them in England until they could afford to marry. They loved the country they served, but lived for their leaves and 'home' and, like my parents, they amused themselves in the evenings by listening to warped gramophone records of the musical shows they had seen at 'home'. It was these young men Somerset Maugham had visited and who were only too glad to talk to him in their loneliness.

We drove down to John's house through miles and miles of jungle, and stayed the night at a remote rest house. There was a marauding tiger in the district, the kapok which filled our pillows had been eaten by hard little beetles who, to our horror, moved away from our heads as soon as we lay down, and our two little dogs, Rosamund's rough-haired fox terrier, Mickey, and my smooth-haired one, James Henry, decided to fight most of the night through our individual mosquito nets.

At John's place, there was an enchanting baby Malayan honey bear called Miss Awang, who was absolutely tame, loved chocolates and honey, but alas dug her own grave by tearing up the tyres on the staff's bicycle wheels and one day she was found poisoned.

We went with John on many of his rounds, chugging up the huge brown crocodile-infested river in a small shabby boat, the river banks bordered with mangroves, their curious knotted roots twisting out of the mud like snakes. While John visited the head men in their long wooden houses on stilts, with attap roofs and spacious verandahs, we were left with the women. The Malay kampongs were charming, set among the coconut palms. Several of the villagers had tame monkeys who were sent shinning up the palms to knock down the ripe coconuts. We also went with John to judge the rice in the paddy fields and, in the evenings, like everyone else, we listened to gramophone records.

Although at Fraser's Hill I used the jungle path from the school to the golf course area nearly every day and most nights, in all the time I was in Malaya I saw very few wild animals – except for crocodiles in the rivers, a tapir and her offspring in Pahang, and a huge jungle tortoise near the school. Snakes were more common. Occasionally on a hot day one of them would come into the cool little bathrooms at St Margaret's up the open plug hole, and the school tukan ayer would take it away. Once or twice there was a small sealing wax snake in the wood pile, and as already mentioned, our fox terrier Jane had flushed some out under our house in Kuala Lumpur, but three main sightings remain in my memory.

I was having a private biology lesson in Kuala Lumpur and the teacher was smelling powerfully of sweat. We were dissecting a cockroach which (as all cockroaches do when killed) was giving out a high sweet pungent smell, when directly beside me on the rattan sofa a cobra appeared through the hole in the arm-rest meant for a whisky glass. It was a great shock!

A friend who lived on an oil palm estate in Johore was with his workers one day when a python attacked him by trying to bite his foot. A python is not poisonous because its way of killing its prey is by winding its tail round a tree trunk and using the rest of its length and strength to squeeze its victim to death, so this one must have been surprised and frightened to have behaved in this way. It was nearly twenty feet long and had strong jaws and teeth. It buried its teeth in the rubber of Jack's boot and couldn't withdraw them. Highly excited, the workers placed a forked stick behind its head, trussed it up and with one man every four feet or so, carried it back to Jack's bungalow. It was crated (curled up it had no power) and deposited in Jack's dining-room which had two wooden walls and two made of wire mesh mosquito netting. Jack received an excellent offer for it from an Irish zoo, so decided to celebrate with some friends on the verandah next to the dining-room. After several drinks, someone suggested that the snake should be let out of the cage for inspection, and Jack agreed. He undid the crate and ran back to the verandah. The snake slithered out and slowly at first but with accelerating speed it inspected its surroundings. Realising that it was still trapped, it began banging violently at the walls and netting, travelling at a tremendous rate. The door and wooden walls began to give and Jack had no choice but to shoot it before it broke up the bungalow.

The third memory is for me the strangest. My headmistress became ill and had to go to hospital. As I was the only assistant, I was now left to run the school by myself but with a cook, his wife who cleaned, and a tukan ayer. I taught all the children from four upwards in the large room at the far end of the building. (I ran the first comprehensive!) The children in groups learned different subjects. The little ones were learning to read and draw, the elder ones were learning geography and we were studying maps dominated by the British Empire coloured in red. Suddenly a cobra glided through the open French window into the room. Cobras in many countries are considered messengers from the gods. I told the children softly to stand on their chairs and not move or speak, and sent the boy nearest the door for the tukan ayer who arrived quickly with fire tongs. He gripped the snake behind its head and removed it. For no particular reason this seemed to me an omen that the Empire was to end soon.

On the Hill scorpions, which in the plains were only an inch or two long, grew to the size of black lobsters. I had a frightening experience trying to kill one in the bedroom I shared with three small children – finally knocking it off the wall on to the floor where I threw a huge book on top of it and stood on the book. Centipedes also grew very large on the Hill and the wretched harmless millipedes, which looked like six-inch tube trains, were always being hacked to death by frightened golfers who thought they were dangerous.

When Rosamund left for her new school, her car went with her, so from then on if I wanted to go to Kuala Lumpur I used the fish car from the Hill, and if I wanted to go on to Singapore, a Chinese mail car. The fish car was very cheap as it brought fish up the hill on ice blocks and went back empty but stinking. Not many other people wanted to use it. The Chinese mail car delivered newspapers. The journey started with tea in the driver's house, where the rest of the passengers met, then they were put in the back and I sat in the front. At a signal along the way the driver would slow down and I threw out a pile of papers.

My father's probationary judgeship was not confirmed and he found a job with the very first firm that had employed him in Singapore. It must have been a bitter blow for him.

Life at the school was harder work now as there were only two of us, and I taught everything but Scripture, maths and (usually) geography. I also played the children into prayers and played the hymns from a very limited repertoire and produced the end of term school plays. I wrote several pop songs at this time. One had the rather catchy title of 'You Tickle Me Spitless Baby', and another 'The Bank Clerk's Blues' was played by the best band in Kuala Lumpur and relayed over the air to some acclaim.

My salary had been slightly increased but I was still very badly paid. As I had my board and lodging free and there were few distractions on the Hill, I wanted for nothing except clothes. Kind friends gave me their cast-offs and I made a couple of dresses for myself but, unlike my mother, I was no needlewoman. I also made my underclothes. To make brassières I folded two men's handkerchiefs into triangles and sewed them up, then crossed over two of the points on the long sides and sewed this to make the cups. With hooks and eyes as fasteners and narrow ribbons as straps they were quite serviceable. But I didn't enjoy having to accept cast-off clothing, and to make more money wrote to the *Malaya Tribune* and suggested that I should write an anonymous weekly gossip column about Fraser's Hill. As it was a holiday station there was a great deal of coming and going and, as there were other columns in the paper called 'Our Singapore Notes', 'Our Kuala Lumpur Notes', and 'Our Penang Notes', it made sense. The editor accepted my idea and offered me three times what I was getting in salary, for 'Our Fraser's Hill Notes'; a few hours' work against a working day of roughly twelve hours! It was manna from heaven! Years and years later Eamonn Andrews asked me to be on Noel Barber's *This is Your Life* on television, having discovered that Noel had been the editor of the *Malaya Tribune* who had accepted my articles! Although we had met and were friends, we had never discovered this connection. I had forgotten the name of the generous editor and, even if he had remembered mine, I had changed it when I became an actress.

 6

My boyfriends multiplied as Fraser's Hill was a holiday centre, but one was the joker in the pack. Few girls slept around in those days because, among other things, knowledge of contraceptives was minimal and, in my case, non-existent. But one of my friends, a customs officer, kept on trying to make me go to bed with him and at last became impatient. At one of the Saturday dances at the Club, he gave me what appeared to be a chocolate truffle after dinner. It was bitter to taste and I exclaimed. To my amazement he kicked me under the table. Something odd seemed to happen to my vision and I felt sick and hurried to the lavatory. On the way back to the school afterwards, I demanded to know what he'd given me. Apparently it was opium. (I had always thought you smoked opium not ate it.) Another time he gave me a hashish cigarette when we were parked on the school drive, going back after the dance. I was sick again, this time all over his car, so mercifully he stopped that form of persuasion. I saw considerably less of him after that and became engaged to one of his colleagues, a charming and good-looking young customs officer called John, whose father had been one of the top detectives, then called the 'Big Four', at Scotland Yard. We were romantically in love with each other and Fraser's Hill is a very romantic place in which to fall in love.

My mother wrote to say that she and my father were coming up the Hill on holiday, but tragically the very next day he was killed in an accident in Singapore harbour. They had gone on board a liner to see some friends off to England, and one of the two gangways for visitors had been removed, but the rail had not been replaced. There was a tremendous crowd. My father stepped back to allow people to pass and, in front of my horrified mother, fell backwards off the ship and landed in the water between the ship and the quay, hitting his head on the quay. He was killed instantly.

My father's last year was extraordinarily neat in its pattern. He was back in his first job in Malaya, he went on leave and stayed with his favourite brother, my godfather, Uncle Jum, and did all the things he most enjoyed – cricket in England and fishing and shooting – then went back to Malaya to Mummy and was delighted to make fifty runs for the 'Non-benders' in a cricket match in Singapore. He died very quickly and the accident moved me deeply. A few years later my mother was to have just such a 'neat' prelude to her own death.

Now she found herself faced with enormous debts. With typical resourcefulness and courage, she landed a job as librarian in the State Library in Singapore, and moved to a very small maisonette in Orchard Road. Her loyal old ayah went with her, and the ayah's husband, who had come back from Mecca as a hadji or holy man, became my mother's 'boy'.

And now came an offer that was radically to change my life. Although I loved Malaya, I felt the lack of any intellectual stimulation and, although I loved my fiancé, I dreaded spending my whole life 'out East', playing bridge or mah-jongg, tennis or badminton. Swimming at night on the long white beaches of the East Coast in phosphorescent seas or dining at Raffles, were beguiling, but to be a mem-sahib with servants to do everything and almost no responsibility didn't lure me so, when a friend, Joyce Green, offered me the job of looking after her two-year-old son on a Danish cargo boat sailing for England, I leapt at the chance.

My fiancé John travelled with me as far as Penang and was due to go home on leave a few weeks later. I don't know if I kidded myself that I also was only going back for a visit. It meant leaving my mother at a difficult time for her, but I wasn't near her up Fraser's Hill and anyway she was fully occupied with her new librarianship post.

But before I went, she and I had an extraordinary and very happy farewell trip together up the Indragiri River in Sumatra. My mother loved the East even more than I, and in fact planned to retire at Cameron Highlands, where shortly she would buy a plot of land. She also loved travel, so she booked us both on a small Dutch river steamer which plied to and from a place called Rengat.

We were the only European women on board. The captain and crew were Dutch and the captain would have been a perfect subject for Conrad or Maugham. He was very idle and rather fat. His face was bloated and his eyes blue and so deep set that it was a surprise to realise that he could actually see through them. He wore dirty white pyjamas all the time on which, during the day, he pinned captain's epaulettes, but he was kind and let me steer the steamer on easy stretches. He felt the heat badly and disliked his job, but probably would have disliked all jobs in such heat. He ate enormous Dutch curries, drank a lot of Bols gin and, to pass the time, shot at the monkeys in the trees by the river with an air gun. The monkey who was struck would look at the suddenly painful spot in apparent amazement, then set to and berate the next monkey on the branch. This was the only thing that made the captain smile.

My last engagement in Singapore was to be a bridesmaid at Rosamund's wedding to a high-up official in the Shell Company. My mother had had two suits made for me as a surprise – one lightweight and the other in thick tweed for England. Because she had no room to put me up, I spent my last night in Singapore with friends called Alfred and Christine Bundy.

When I went to bed I put sixty pounds, all I had in the world, under my pillow and settled down to sleep under the mosquito net.

My bed was on the verandah and all the chicks (light straw roller blinds) were down. Some time later I awoke in terror to see the chick at the foot of my bed being slowly drawn up, then a Chinaman, clearly outlined in the moonlight, climbed over the verandah rail and headed straight towards me. At this moment the Bundys' two dogs rushed in, under the high wooden swing doors of my room, barking wildly. The man disappeared with the dogs chasing after him, and the Bundys rushed in to see what had happened. I told them and they said, 'Why didn't you scream?' Astonished, I said that I did. I had a clear recollection of sitting bolt upright and screaming.

'Not a sound,' they said. 'You were lying down in complete silence when we arrived.'

7

There are certain decisions which change the entire course of our lives. Most people, if they think about it at all, believe that we have a choice; but there is a determined minority who believe that all is planned by some omniscient being. I incline to the latter view, but not wholeheartedly. The most I will admit is that a pattern is sometimes discernible, an intimation of the future, like a butterfly may experience when it is a chrysalis, or that we may see in dreams.

Chuang Chou, in his thoughts on death from his *Three Ways of Thought of Ancient China* (translated from the Chinese by Arthur Waley), says:

. . . How do we know that wanting to be alive is not a great mistake? How do I know that hating to die is not like thinking one has lost one's way, when all the time one is on the path to home? . . . While a man is dreaming, he does not know that he is dreaming, nor can he interpret his dream until the dream is done . . . Once Chuang Chou dreamt that he was a butterfly, and was content to hover from flower to flower. Suddenly he woke, and found to his astonishment that he was Chou. But it was hard to be sure whether he was really Chou, and had only dreamt that he was a butterfly, or whether he was a butterfly and was only dreaming that he was Chou.

We so often (or I seem to) have these moments of recognition of the past's relation to the present or indeed to the future, that time and chance and free will cease to be individually dominant, and out of the ensuing confusion I search for signs of the pattern which my instincts tell me will help me to make the right decision, or at least to understand.

The sequence of events which followed my trip to England and which resulted in my becoming an actress would seem almost too farfetched had there not been some predestined pattern. Few men will approve of such a theory, although H. G. Wells did. Many women will accept it. There was little sign of it at first.

Joyce Green was the perfect employer. She wasn't offering me wealth, in fact I had to pay her thirty pounds of my precious sixty pounds as part of the fare, but she was kind, thoughtful and a wonderful companion. Only in her twenties herself, she had huge grey eyes, a turned-up nose, a very smooth skin and she was always laughing. She left me to look after two-year-old Jeremy without interference, and never once condescended to me. She was naturally taken up with her new baby Celia and was going back to her family home in County Clare to introduce the children to their grandmother. Her husband 'Squirrel' was to follow her shortly. Actually Joyce reminded me of a squirrel.

Besides my one thick suit for England, I had knitted two long-sleeved sweaters and had bought two cheap skirts from an English catalogue. I had several cast-off evening dresses and of course summer clothes. But most important of all, Auntie Hedges, my old head-mistress from St Anthony's, Wallingford, had offered me a job at the school.

The Danish cargo ship had cabins for a few passengers. Besides Joyce and me and her children, there was a Frenchman who was so sea-sick that although he started every meal with us, he usually left with his napkin held close to his mouth and his eyes rolling before he had eaten almost anything, and a honeymoon couple from Lancashire who used toothpicks ferociously behind their napkins and looked deep into each other's eyes, went scarlet and then burst into silent laughter. But at Colombo we took on our star.

She was English of Italian extraction and she had a little boy of four years old. Her husband, a tea planter from a remote plantation, was sending her back to England because she had created a scandal. Bored to distraction she had taken a lover who, in a moment of frenzy tried to shoot her husband, but missed. Surprised but magnanimous the husband agreed to forget the whole incident, as long as the lover stopped seeing his wife, which he thankfully agreed to do. All would now have been well, had not the wife claimed to have had a headache one day, and the husband, ever solicitous, offered to fetch her an aspirin. In the pill box, lovingly preserved, he found the bullet that had been meant to kill him. Angry at last, he despatched her back to her family with their little boy. In Colombo, however, outraged at her dismissal, the lady called a conference to tell the press her exciting news. The police reacted swiftly and, even before she left, to her horror they had arrested the lover. This she told us each in turn and swore us all to ineffectual secrecy. She was popular only as a story teller.

She dressed for the hot evenings in black velvet with a cleavage in which nestled a moonstone cross. She powdered heavily and dramatically with a dead white powder and her small mouth was made up crimson. She fell for the ship's doctor, who was flirting mildly with me, and battled for his attention by pretending to be ill. She treated me like a skivvy and her very badly behaved little four-year-old actually bit Jeremy more than once. I bit him in return (not too hard) and dramas ensued. At the various ports she attempted to leave her child with me while she went ashore, but I refused and she became a virago.

We called at Djibouti which was buzzing with the news of Mussolini's invasion of Abyssinia. We called at Aden where we heard gossip about King Edward VIII and Mrs Simpson; in fact we heard far more than the British public knew or, of course, than we had heard in Malaya.

The voyage lasted six weeks. Jeremy took up most of the daylight hours. He was a charming little boy and not much trouble but I had a terrible time trying to keep his rompers clean. I had to wash them myself as part of the job. I had never had to launder anything in my life before, even at Fraser's Hill, and had no idea sea water and soap were not a good combination. Although I scrubbed hard, all the garments turned a depressing grey before the journey ended and, despite attempts to iron them, they always looked creased.

The days began far too early because the only time Jeremy could be allowed to play on deck in the Indian Ocean or the Red Sea was before the sun had reached full strength. We shared a clean, comfortable little cabin with a bathroom, but bathing him, if there was a sea running, was another difficulty. If it was too rough I felt sick and had to lie down from time to time. To this Jeremy became used, so that on a calm day he would often say 'Perghil tidor' (pronounced piggy teedor) which meant 'Go to sleep.' He called me 'Ardy', a mixture I suppose of Auntie and Amah and it made me think of Nelson, when at night he used to say 'Tiss me Ardy,' and I kissed him.

We reached Tilbury and England in a fog so thick we could hardly see our hands in front of our faces. It was raw and cold and very unattractive, but we found a taxi and as both Joyce and I were heading for Earl's Court we shared it. Joyce was to leave for Ireland with the children later in the week, and I was to spend three weeks with my mother's brother, his wife and their daughters.

The spirit of London was very different at that time. Although the 'thirties were a time of deep depression, the city took itself seriously as the world's greatest capital. People dressed up to go out with hats and gloves, and most smart women wore black with pearls, and silver fox furs draped round their shoulders. So did the tarts, then often seen on the streets holding black poodles on leads. There was no litter and men accompanying women still walked on the outside of the pavements to protect them from harm, and from the dirt from the traffic. But ex-servicemen, veterans of the Great War, sometimes with an arm or leg missing and wearing their medals, sold matches in the streets.

There were traffic jams even then, although private cars were comparatively few. Taxis had ranks with telephone numbers and could be ordered, with fares starting at 6d. High-class shops had little vans, usually bearing the Royal Arms 'By Appointment', drawn by small, beautifully groomed ponies, and huge carthorses with plaited manes pulled the brewers' drays.

One day I was walking up Piccadilly towards Hyde Park Corner on the opposite side from the Ritz when a slim, beautifully dressed woman with a huge diamond brooch, a choker of pearls and a thin, hard, crimson lipsticked mouth came towards me. She had bony legs and very high-heeled shoes. She created a small sensation and, when I asked why, I was told she was Mrs Simpson. Shortly afterwards, with the friend to whom I'd sold my lacrosse stick before leaving for Malaya, I heard the Abdication Speech. I was horrified because, being a Colonial, I had thought the King should put his country first, but I was also touched because it seemed a wonderful love story. I was amazed however that it was that tough little lady who had inspired such love. I wrote and told my mother about it, and she wrote back to say she was not at all surprised as they had had the Prince of Wales to stay in Kuala Lumpur on his world tour, and had found him a difficult guest. He would be out until all hours with highly unsuitable girlfriends, climbing back into our house by the back, while a 'boy' with whisky and sandwiches was still waiting for him at the front. On his railway journey through the country, he often slept through stations where loyal crowds were waiting for a glimpse of him. As an ardent monarchist, my mother had been clearly shocked.

I was fascinated by London, but also homesick and cold. My cousins were charming to me, but we had led very different lives and I was kindly advised by friends, for my own sake, not to talk of Kuala Lumpur or the fact that I was a schoolmistress, because it would be considered socially farouche.

This was November 1936, and my job at St Anthony's was to start in January. In the interim I stayed with various kindly aunts and it was while playing with a young cousin at Aunt Gemma's in Oxford that I managed to break my wrist. It meant that I couldn't take up my post with Auntie Hedges in Wallingford because she had been relying on me supervising energetic activities like games and gym.

I was devastated. Aunt Gemma and I set about job-hunting for me and found instead an advertisement in *The Times* for three scholarships at the studio of Amédée Ozenfant at the École des Beaux Arts in the Warwick Road, London. He was a surrealist painter of some repute; and Aunt Gemma's sister, Mary McDowall, who was a painter herself, much approved of him. I sat for the scholarships with, among others, two highly talented Scots girls. I won one of the three places. The prize was a small allowance and free tuition. Extraordinary that Mummy's ambition for me to paint had in such a roundabout way been fulfilled!

I spent three months with Ozenfant. He and a friend who painted under the name of Jeanneret had founded a movement in about 1915 called the Purists of Paris. Their peak period of influence was in the decade 1917–27. They influenced Matisse considerably and one of Ozenfant's pupils was Fernand Léger, with whom Ozenfant became very disillusioned when Léger 'plagiarised' his teacher's ideas and became highly successful with them. Ozenfant also accused Calder of usurping his (Ozenfant's) claim to be the inventor of mobiles. Eventually Jeanneret stopped painting and became world famous as the architect Le Corbusier. Ozenfant continued on his own.

By the time I reached him, he was in his middle fifties or sixties. He had wiry grey hair, looked like a parrot and wore a smock and sneakers. He had a blonde Scandinavian assistant at the studios, who we all decided was his mistress.

The studio was small with a little entrance in which hung one of his mobiles, a room to the left which was used as an overflow for students' exhibitions and a dressing-room for the models. The main room where we all worked was lit by a large skylight and heated by a tall coke-burning stove. It was divided by a curtain from where Ozenfant was working on a large picture called *Vie* which nearly covered the back wall. This is now in the Metropolitan in New York, an oil on canvas, painted with a sable brush which took him six years to finish. It was crowded with gesticulating people and, when I was there, was developing in colour from grey blue to mauve. Many years after his death, the Tate held an exhibition called 'The Purists of Paris', which would have delighted him.

The pupils assembled at ten in the morning. The maître was already at work. Mornings were devoted to drawing, the afternoon to painting, but painting was a reward only for those who had obtained his approbation that morning. The technique he imposed on us was rigid. We used Double Elephant Medium paper, medium soft pencils and soft rubbers for drawing. The tempo was extremely slow and rubbing out was encouraged. Pure line was to relate to pure line, but 'perfect in form of itself'. If this led to distortion of the object drawn, it was unimportant to him. Design was all, and 'petitisms' (areas too small to be significant) were frowned on. For painting we used sable brushes as he did, and painted in rectangles, first horizontally, then up and down to achieve perfect smoothness. We had a chart on the wall to show us the only colours we were permitted to use.

In the main room, there was a trestle table on which the model posed and, as he (or she) was very near the stove, he also posed problems to painters in the winter by becoming scarlet on the side nearest the stove, and remaining blue with cold on the other. The stove doubled as a cooker. Those of us who were hard up used it for our lunch of scrambled eggs, sausages and bacon. The only other students I remember were two male Egyptians, two elderly ladies and the other two scholarship girls.

At midday the studio was open to the astonished public – surrealism was new in England then – and Ozenfant, now dressed in a blue suit but still with his dirty sneakers, threw back his curtain and came gravely into our part of the room to give us all his considered opinions. He was always very kind to me, chiefly I think because I spoke a courageous Churchillian French to him, and he felt very much an exile in England. Our pictures were on sale, and I often sold my works for small sums which was a godsend.

Ozenfant was kind to me outside the studio too. He was a great friend of the sculptor Jacob Epstein, who had a house in Hyde Park Gate, and on Sundays he took me to tea there. Epstein, a thickset heavy man with strong grey hair and a boxer's face, supplied me with huge high teas which his wife and daughter used to make. It seems extraordinary now but he was having a very difficult time, and was frequently reviled for being controversial. His sculpture *Rima* was later bought to be a laughter-making sideshow at Blackpool. Amazing! His *Christ in Majesty* in Llandaff cathedral and his *Virgin and Child* in Cavendish Square are surely great works by any standards, not to mention those marvellous portrait busts.

Epstein was painting water colours at this period, all priced at sixty pounds. How I wish I could have bought one! He had painted sixty water colours of Epping Forest and sixty of magnificently vivid red and striped tulips, usually painted looking right into the cup, with the black stamens strongly depicted. I browsed alone in his studio for hours. I only wish I had been more knowledgeable about painting and sculpture then. What an opportunity to lose because I was so recently from the jungle!

Winning that scholarship had another side effect that was entirely beneficial. I had no proper winter coat and to buy one was impossible. Feeling the cold as I did was an agony, but because of Ozenfant and indeed of Epstein, I discovered picture galleries. They were free, all except the Leicester Gallery which cost 1/6d, they were warm and however often I turned up I was welcome. Also they contained beauty. At the Storran Galleries opposite Harrods, there was an exhibition by Modigliani, with the pictures priced at £100. Soon I wanted one of them, too, although at first I almost found them ridiculous. I spent a week in the gallery and gradually not only did I become more and more enamoured, but everyone in the outside world became a Modigliani with long necks, thin wandering noses, high colouring and small eyes.

I was staying in a 15s (75p) a week flat in Edith Road, which Auntie D had found for me, and felt that I ought to take up the introductions I had had from my mother to two of her friends. None of my family had seemed to be too shocked at my new life style, so although these friends had not troubled to get in touch with me, I plucked up my courage and invited them both to tea.

I had really quite an attractive bed-sitting room, although the district was by no means fashionable. My room was at the back of the apartment block and had a large window overlooking an ill-kept lawn, but with a lovely plane tree. I had a bed with a light green coverlet which matched the curtains, a round table in the centre, two hard chairs and a small rectangular table against the wall all of fumed oak. There was a gas fire with a meter, a wardrobe for my clothes and a large cupboard for everything else. The bathroom, for all the lodgers but Auntie D (who had her own), was just outside my bedroom on the half-landing. It had a geyser in it on which was written 'Boiling in two minutes'.

I bought bread and butter, jam, some tea, cakes, milk and sugar, and a small tea service from Woolworths, each piece costing 6d. Everything in Woolworths cost 6d then. Flowers seemed too expensive so I bought a goldfish bowl for 6d, and a goldfish for 6d. I thought anyway that the fish would last longer than flowers, and to cheer up the walls I put up some of my drawings of nudes.

My two guests were a Brigadier General and an Australian woman who had been a beauty queen, and neither were happy about coming to such a district. My drawings embarrassed them, especially a full frontal of a powerful negro, and as the bed was the only comfortable thing in the room, I put them on it side by side, and they had never met before. The tea made with water heated for two minutes precisely from the geyser was a greyish concoction with the leaves floating on top (I had never made tea). The conversation did not flow and they couldn't look at the pictures which shocked them deeply. They couldn't drink the tea either, and their proximity on the bed alarmed them.

I never saw either of them again.

My fiancé had by now arrived in England and was, not surprisingly, disconcerted by my circumstances. He didn't understand why I was studying painting if I was going to go back to Malaya with him. I can't remember now what excuse I gave, but it seemed to satisfy him. We had good times together. We went to the Coronation of King George VI and Queen Elizabeth (now the Queen Mother), and as Colonials had excellent seats on the tiered stands to the right of Buckingham Palace. We cheered everyone and everything, especially the Malay Sultans. We went to the Café de Paris, then one of the smartest places in London, and the Café Anglais, nearby in Leicester Square but down-market, and there I met a head girl from one of my schools who was dancing with an old man. In the cloakroom she told me I was a lucky bitch to be dancing with a young and handsome man, instead of a Sugar Daddy. I told her it was rather sweet of her father to be so kind and she nearly hit me. She later became a full-time prostitute. I saw her one night with a black poodle on her pitch opposite the Ritz, and she not surprisingly cut me dead. Later still she married very respectably.

I was in a dilemma about my engagement. John was clever, kind and an excellent companion. We never quarrelled and I had a great respect and admiration as well as affection for him, but it wasn't enough. I knew with all my heart that I wanted to stay in England. Every time I was with him I felt a traitor but I didn't want to ruin his leave by telling him we had no future. I knew only too well how important his leave was to him.

And then my old schoolfriend Jane Boulenger came back into my life with a proposition.

8

My time at Ozenfant's was coming to an end, and I was wondering what to do next. There were not many jobs going for my kind of woman in those days, except being a governess, teaching in a kindergarten, or being companion to an old lady. The girl who had taken my place at St Anthony's was satisfactory and had therefore been kept on, and if I was really to stay in England, I must get work.

Jane had been going to be an actress, but when she was cast in a play at the Webber Douglas drama school as Stewart Granger's mother (and he was considerably older than she), she felt she was in the wrong business and became the secretary of the school instead.

We had already had one or two meals together since my return to England, at Lyons or the ABC, the cheap places in those days. She asked me if I thought I could exist as a full-time painter and I said that with so little training and probably only a talent, not a gift, I thought not. Besides, in spite of my mother's hopes for me and, although I had revelled in my life at Ozenfant's, I knew that a painter's life was not for me, so Jane suggested I should try for a place at the Webber Douglas where auditions for a scholarship were to be held quite soon. As the thought of being an actress had never occurred to me, I had absolutely nothing to lose, so I applied.

The Webber Douglas is still in Clareville Grove off Gloucester Road, and the room where the auditions were to be held was in the school basement – a large room with a wooden floor and on this occasion a small rostrum had been set up at one end. Mr Douglas, Ellen O'Malley and Carina Thorburn (the main secretary) were the adjudicators.

Ellen O'Malley had been a well-known actress. She was a great friend of Bernard Shaw's and he had written the part of Ellie Dunn in *Heartbreak House* for her. By the time I knew her, she was a voluminous, expansive, white-haired old woman with a deep voice, and her style of acting was broad and old-fashioned but blazingly truthful as well.

For my Shakespeare piece for the audition I gave them 'The quality of mercy is not strained' in the hopes that they would, indeed, be merciful. I was, and am, very shy but as I took my place on the rostrum my shyness went and I felt completely at home. It was a strange and exhilarating feeling and I won the scholarship.

The stage is the perfect place for a shy person. You are lit to the best advantage and clothed to the best advantage. The words you speak have (usually!) been carefully crafted. You know when to come into the room and when to leave. You know to whom you are to speak and whom you will meet. Further you have rehearsed under direction, the exact way in which you are to say what you have to say.

In the event they changed their minds about the scholarship for me, and gave it to Barbara Mullen, whose father had just made a film called *Man of Arran* which was a critical success. Babs was as broke as I was, but being her father's daughter she was also a good advertisement for the school which was still in its infancy. I was offered reduced fees, £15 a term. But how on earth was I to pay? At this point a small legacy from one of my great-aunts came my way – one third of an eighty-fourth share of her estate – £300.

It was extraordinary how things had worked out for me, Joyce, Ozenfant and now my great-aunt! It seemed as if my whole life had been a wayward prelude to becoming an actress. I had never been happier.

Being a student is wonderfully exciting. The great world round the corner seems yours for the taking. I had to be frugal of course if the money was to last. I needed books – the complete works of Shakespeare for a start. I needed clothes for dancing and fencing, and I decided to move nearer the school so that I could walk to it if need be. In this I was lucky. I found another room, small but spotless, in a newly converted house in Kempsford Gardens. Everything was going to be all right!

The work utterly absorbed me and most of the other pupils were friendly. We were a strange lot. There were seventy-five girls and seven men. (Acting was not considered a manly profession then.) The girls were divided sharply between the haves and have nots. Many were debutantes using the Webber Douglas as a finishing school. (One was in deep trouble with her family because she had been dancing naked down the corridor at home at breakfast time, and had run into the butler who had then had to be sacked because he had seen her without her clothes on. As he was an excellent butler, she was not popular.) They were all very generous however, and I was invited to many of their homes for the meals they knew I needed. One of them, Anne Somerset, one of the prettiest redheads I have ever seen, was especially concerned, and her aunt and uncle Blanchie and Leo Lonsdale often had me to meals or to stay in their lovely house in Great Cumberland Place and treated me with great kindness.

Another pretty girl, Betty Lee, whose mother had married again and was now Lady Rossmore, invited me to several splendid parties where, among others, I met Joseph Kennedy (father of John F. and Robert), the United States Ambassador to this country – a weasel-faced Irishman who had a contemptuous hatred for England – and his handsome wife Rose.

Perhaps the most bizarre help came from a student who had left the school to become social secretary to a Conservative MP who gave large luncheon parties at the Ritz. The luncheons were in order to make useful friends and impress people. By some magic, my friend Helen saw to it that I was on his list. Although he seemed a little puzzled that I turned up so frequently, the MP never asked me why I was there and, except for some charming nothings at the beginning and end of the meals, he never took any interest in me.

Many years later when I was living in Dolphin Square, I met him in the lift at Nelson House. He half recognised me but had luckily forgotten that I had been his guest so often. I, who was immensely grateful to him, was perhaps over-enthusiastic in my greetings, with the result that he pursued me ardently for the rest of that summer and one of the tokens of his affection were a series of single chocolates in my letter box with a note saying 'Sweets to the sweet' and other flattering messages. As it was a hot summer, the chocolates tended to melt over my other mail and I grew a little harassed until he turned his affection elsewhere.

With one of the other impoverished girls, I shared the same lunch every day at the ABC in the Gloucester Road. We had between us a small 8d meat pie, vegetables 2d and potatoes 2d – 6d per day and sometimes it would be all I had for several days running.

The holidays were a problem for me. That first summer I stayed in Ireland with Joyce Green for three weeks. We sailed in a centre-board regatta on Loch Derg and stayed at her mother's beautiful eighteenth-century house at Mount Shannon. I also found some jobs to help with the financial situation. I taught a Spanish girl English and an Italian girl English, and walked Ellen O'Malley's arthritic little fox terrier,

Tim, once a week. (He hated walking and used to hide from me under the grandfather clock in the hall. Ellen's little maid, dressed in a chocolate brown uniform, with a biscuit coloured cap and apron, loved this part of the performance. I was the only person she ever met who was, she felt, lower down the social scale.) I wrote letters for the British Road Federation, too, a body dedicated to beautifying British roads. Funnily enough the A40, on which I travel almost daily, was one of the roads we 'beautified' and very slight traces of our ideas still remain. When desperate, I also took on one or two modelling jobs at art schools and with artists.

Modelling is one of the least pleasant jobs I know, clothed or unclothed. Being nude isn't the trouble, certainly not with students. One is anonymous as far as they are concerned, and as they are there to do a job, as one is oneself, one rapidly learns not to be self-conscious. Staying in one position is agony. Until one learns how to save oneself, one has cramps, aches in the joints and exhaustion. Standing is obviously the worst, but resting on an elbow, taking up a position with an arm outstretched or with one's back twisted even in a minor degree, can be painful in the extreme. Some painters could be and sometimes were a bore, but if they were, I simply didn't turn up again. But the cold! That was the worst of all things.

I modelled for two weeks for Mary McDowall, Aunt Gemma's artist sister, and two friends of hers at her house at Idstone in Berkshire. The three women, who had been at the Slade together years before, had now grown away from one another. They quarrelled a great deal of the time and I could shift my position and be sure that, if one complained, another would say I hadn't moved, just to be awkward to the other. I was there for my board and keep and whatever pay they deemed fit. The richest of the three was the meanest. I used to be sent out to collect mushrooms for supper while taking the highly strung spaniel, Patrick, for a walk. He used to have fits and, when he did, the only way I could get him home was to wrap him up in my mackintosh and carry him. Unconscious, he was enormously heavy.

The time came for my long-suffering fiancé to leave again for Malaya and I saw him off at Liverpool. I'm sure we both knew by this time that we would never marry. I wrote and told him so a few weeks after he left. I still much regret my behaviour. He didn't deserve it and I didn't deserve such kindness. I still see him sometimes, I'm glad to say.

One learns more in a week of acting professionally than in a whole two years at a drama school. But it is nevertheless good for the basics. One learns to move, how to use theatre make-up, how to breathe properly and how to use one's voice, and one is part of a group of people for whom the theatre is the most important thing in the world.

The make-up then was very different from now. Footlights were still used in theatres; a row of coloured lights at ground level at the front of the stage, and they were very flattering. By some extraordinary mistake, one night when we were performing *An Ideal Husband* at the Strand Theatre in the 'sixties, someone put on the footlights and all of us thoroughly enjoyed them! They distanced the audience and made us feel enclosed in the reality of the story we were telling.

In those days there were no lighting experts. The foundation for a 'straight' make-up for women was a mixture of two sticks of Leichner make-up, colours 5 and 9 mixed. This gave a slightly rosy sunburnt look. We used a thinner stick of Carmine 2 for cheeks and lips (although there was Carmine 2 powder rouge for those who preferred it). A thin blue stick was used for the eyelids, the blue taken right up to the eyebrows, and the eyes were outlined with a black liner, with carmine dots near the nose and by the outer corners. On the top and bottom lids, the lines carried on beyond the eye and themselves were lined with white, as also was the inside edge of the lower lids. False eyelashes had only just been invented. Most people used hot black. This was a thick black stick of make-up which looked like a black candle. A scrape of it was heated in a tea spoon over a real candle and it spluttered and fizzed as it became liquid. With an orange-stick you dropped drops of the liquid on to your eyelashes, where they stayed as thick blobs. If you missed the eyelashes and the liquid fell on the cheeks, it made a black smear which often meant a re-make-up. We were told that the great ladies of the immediate past, Ellen Terry, Yvonne Arnaud and Marie Tempest, used to rouge the lobes of their ears, their elbows and their fingertips, and wet-white their hands and arms. Wet white came out of a bottle in various pale colours and was wiped on bare arms and legs. Dancers used wet white and in the gents' lavatory at home, we have a list of instructions which used to hang in all the dressing-rooms of the Chelsea Palace Theatre. One reads:

WARNING [this in red capitals]
Very serious accidents have happened to artistes by standing in Wash Basins to remove 'wet white'. The basins collapsed and THE GIRLS WERE TERRIBLY LACERATED. [black capitals]

By the time I reached the stage we didn't bother about wet white, nor about rouge on ear lobes, elbows or fingertips! Strangely enough, even heavy stage make-up doesn't harm the skin if it is carefully removed with a good remover or with old-fashioned Crow's Cremine, although nowadays one only uses a slightly more defined street make-up, except for character parts. Those great actors Henry Irving and Laurence Olivier used water colour for special make-up effects – Larry with outstanding success, I remember, in *Titus Andronicus*. I have never heard of anyone else doing so. Irving was the first actor to be knighted and Olivier the first actor to be made a peer. It is intriguing that they should also have had water colour in common!

Besides Ellen O'Malley and Audrey Bullard, our voice teacher, we had as teachers Alison Leggatt who was actually acting with Noël Coward in *Tonight at 8.30* in the West End, Susan Richmond, a very precise character actress with a pointed nose, who was also often in plays in London, and Molly Terraine who was afterwards put in charge of the film starlets at Rank's Charm School. All in their different ways were helpful and encouraging.

9

Michael Denison arrived at the Webber Douglas in my second term. He was extremely good-looking with dark hair and blue eyes, and created a sensation by arriving in a bowler hat and carrying a rolled umbrella. He never brought either again. By chance he had met one of my uncles a few weeks previously, who had told him to look out for me. We met sitting on the low wall that runs across the front of the school, and I remember that we were all eating cherries. I found him almost too good-looking. Besides I was not in the market for emotional entanglements as I had just broken with John, but I soon came to admire his talent as an actor.

His path to drama school was very different from mine. His father was a paint manufacturer from Doncaster and his mother, who died soon after Michael's birth, was the youngest child of a notable figure in Yorkshire business life – diamond prospector, insurance broker and Lord Mayor of Leeds in 1913. (I still wear the ring he had made for his wife on return from the Kimberley diamond rush of 1871.) Michael was brought up devotedly by his mother's eldest sister, and her Scots accountant husband Jack Ballardie who had no children of their own. At boarding school in Broadstairs from the age of eight, Michael won a scholarship to Harrow (where he fagged for Terence Rattigan), and went on to Magdalen College, Oxford. He realised that he wanted to be an actor during an OUDS production of *Richard II*, directed jointly by John Gielgud and Glen Byam Shaw. They were both appearing in John's famous production of *Romeo and Juliet* with Peggy Ashcroft, Laurence Olivier and Edith Evans. Glen went to Oxford each evening after the performance, and John gave them every Sunday and most of Monday. Michael had three tiny parts, the Lord Fitzwater, Sir Stephen Scroop and a herald. Vivien Leigh, the ravishingly beautiful new young actress of the moment, played the Queen. It was the first time Michael had had an inkling of the difference between amateur and professional actors, and it made up his mind for him.

We soon became excellent friends and began to see a lot of one another, but nearly always in a foursome with Nicholas Meredith who shared Michael's digs and another student, Helen Shingler. It wasn't until the end of his second term that we acted together opposite one another. Michael bought white roses for the performance and, as they were very expensive and he wasn't well off, I realised that his feelings were becoming involved, like my own.

For my second summer holiday, I had just got myself a job as a temporary governess when Anne Somerset asked me to play Maria in *School for Scandal* in an amateur production at Stansted, the Bessboroughs' stately home near Chichester. I managed to get out of my governess job and presented myself at Stansted with two new dresses, one costing 2/11d and one 4/11d from a sale in C & A's bargain basement. Lady Bessborough complimented me on one of them and, on hearing how much it cost, said with a charming smile and a twinkling eye, 'You won't see many like it here, my dear,' and I loved her from that moment.

Anne was playing Lady Teazle and Nicholas Meredith Charles Surface, so knowing three of the cast gave Michael the excuse to come to a performance, and he was invited to stay to supper after the show. At supper I sat next to him and we both realised that we were in love.

Stansted was an eye-opener for me. The present house, which was built at the turn of the century in William and Mary style, has inherited its noble setting from the Georgian house destroyed by fire. The rooms are large, high ceilinged and beautifully furnished. The grounds were laid out by Capability Brown with three great avenues radiating from the house beyond a lawn large enough for cricket matches. The Georgian stables survived the fire and housed the charming little theatre in which we played. (The theatre was later burned down during the war.)

And the food! It was almost reminiscent of Malaya. A huge breakfast was usually taken alone with Vere (Lord and Lady Bessborough had asked me to call them Vere and Roberte, but they were so impressive that I found it hard to do for some time). A large luncheon was followed by tea, and the final dinner or supper. I felt alive and well. Half-starved you don't. You mostly have a headache and stomach cramps. To crown it all, *The Times* gave me an excellent notice for my performance as Maria.

That summer, Michael's much loved uncle Jack Ballardie had a stroke and went bankrupt. He lived on for nine years, paralysed and only able to speak two words, 'My God.' I visited him throughout the war; indeed until he died. We loved one another – but all the time he longed to die. His world was shattered and so was the background of Michael's.

Michael left the Webber Douglas after his third term and was offered three jobs, one at Perranporth repertory company, one to play *Charlie's Aunt* at Frinton, and one at the Westminster. He accepted the last two.

The company at the Westminster was highly distinguished on every level except its capacity to pay a decent salary (he earned £3 a week less half a crown insurance). It was called The London Mask Theatre Company and had been promoted by J. B. Priestley – who became Michael's fairy godfather in the theatre – and Ronald Jeans, another playwright. The artistic director was Michael MacOwan, brilliant and vital, and its stars were Catherine Lacey, Robert Harris, Stephen Murray and Max Adrian. They played Shakespeare, Shaw, O'Neill, Eliot and Priestley, and for Michael, although the company lost money throughout its life, it was an ideal theatrical education. They opened to the background of the Munich crisis with Shakespeare's *Troilus and Cressida*, in which Michael played Paris; then followed with Priestley's *Dangerous Corner*, Michael playing the marvellous part of Gordon in which he made an instant success.

Meanwhile, volunteers were digging pathetic slit trenches in the London parks. Although Chamberlain had announced 'peace in our time', we were all quite prepared in our minds for war and Michael, who had decided at Stansted that he wanted to marry me, wrote me a note on November 10th after we had spent the afternoon skating together at Earl's Court, and left it under the door at Kempsford Gardens, asking me to lunch at the Dorchester Hotel the next day, 'if I felt the same as he did.' On his salary, lunch at the Dorchester was quite an offer! I did feel as he did and we became unofficially engaged.

My mother came on leave for six months. Why she came over in the winter when she felt the cold so keenly, I don't know. Perhaps she thought it might be her only chance. She was enjoying her job as a librarian in Singapore, and had made two startling innovations. She had always wanted to own a crocodile, so installed one in a tank in the courtyard of the library, and when rats invaded the premises, she put down a reticulated python to deal with them.

She was less than enthusiastic about Michael as a suitor as his financial prospects seemed uncertain to say the least, and he had no parents for her to inspect. Also, although she had always been passionately keen on the theatre, she wasn't too keen on either of us being on the stage. She asked him and Nicholas Meredith (who later joined Michael at the Westminster) to cocktails and, with a great air, dispensed Empire Burgundy and soda as the only drink. She was on top form. Both Nick and Michael fell under her extraordinary spell at once, and she liked them both immediately, but she remained very worried.

At Christmas – one of the coldest Christmases I have ever known – she and I went to lodgings in Southwold on the East Coast, by bus, as she had friends there, and there I had a horrific nightmare. I dreamt that we were on a liner in the Indian Ocean and that the liner sank with the passengers screaming, diving overboard, trying to take to the rafts and lifeboats, and some drowning. I ran into her room to tell her and she comforted me. It was a horrible experience I was to relive a couple of years later.

Michael joined us for a few days, wearing some pale blue plus fours which he adored but which didn't suit him. In January my mother went to stay with friends in Antwerp, and on March 11th, 1939, Michael and I became officially engaged. (This meant that it was announced in the papers.)

10

My two years at the Webber Douglas were nearly over and it was my turn to look for a job. In the last term my best part was going to be a sixty-year-old landlady – hardly a good way to catch a prospective employer's eye – but Michael remonstrated and I was given two wonderful parts, Laura in *Still Life* (better known in its film version as *Brief Encounter*) and Rosalind in *As You Like It*.

In the event I was offered the classic one-way ticket to Buenos Aires as a show girl, and the lead twice nightly twice weekly, at Hunstanton.

Meanwhile, Michael had been offered a part (again for a pittance) by Terence Rattigan in his new play for the West End, *After the Dance*, which was to be produced at the end of the Westminster season; and at the same time Rodney Millington who had just started the very successful casting directory, *Spotlight*, offered him a job in a new repertory company to be called A. R. Whatmore's London Players for a summer season in Aberdeen at £9 a week. Financially this last was a great temptation, but Michael's Westminster contract and Terry's offer ruled it out. He went to see Rodney to thank him and explain, adding that he had just become engaged and didn't want to go so far away from me. When Rodney learnt who I was, he said that he had seen me in the end of term shows and had thought very highly of me; so highly indeed that he would offer me £6 a week to join Michael. £15 a week for a guaranteed six weeks' work! We were rich! We could marry, if Ronald Jeans and J. B. Priestley would let Michael out of his Westminster contract! Ronald Jeans immediately agreed, but Priestley couldn't be found. When he was run to earth at the Welcombe Hotel in Stratford-on-Avon, he said, 'Oh, aye, let the lad go. He's done good work for us for tuppence, but tell him we expect him to come back to us in the autumn.'

Dear Jack! What a wonderful friend he was to us. The snide nickname he was given of 'Jolly Jack', because he was supposed to be such a grumbler, never seemed to us to suit him at all. He was a marvellous 'good companion', inventively funny and his small shouts of laughter when he bared his teeth a little and slightly shook his shoulders, his brilliant mimicry of pretentious acquaintances, and his kindness to anyone in trouble, were totally endearing. As his widow Jacquetta Hawkes said after he died, 'He was strangely misunderstood. He was such a sweet fellow.' I agree.

Mummy was still adamantly opposed to our marriage, but we went ahead with the preparations in the hope that she would see reason. Michael got a special licence for the wedding at St Saviour's, Walton Street on the Saturday before we left for Aberdeen at 11 o'clock, because he had his final two performances to give at the Westminster. I bought a blue linen suit for £2 12s 6d (£2.62½), a maroon straw hat 8s 11d (44½p), a speckled maroon and cream blouse 13s 6d (67½p), a long evening dress for the one-night honeymoon, white organdie edged in black, with a black velvet sash £2 12s 6d (£2.62½) and a going-away dress in tweed 15s (75p) – a total trousseau outlay of £7 2s 5d (£7.12). Michael gave me cream and maroon orchids which exactly matched my blouse. He has always had style, even on the bread line. Meanwhile I, too, was rehearsing and packing everything we owned.

We went down to the nursing home at Wimbledon to tell Michael's Uncle Jack the news and he said 'My God!' in a very approving tone. At the last moment Mummy relented and on Saturday, April 29th, at 11 o'clock, in a church filled with flowers for a subsequent wedding, an awning and red carpet provided for yet another couple, and with Uncle Jum to give me away, we were married. On the way back down the aisle, Michael whispered lovingly into my ear, 'One minute on the way to our Golden Wedding.' I have never felt so tired!

My beloved Auntie Pat and Uncle Clu gave a reception. Mummy left for a weekend with friends in the country. (It was the last time I ever saw her.) Michael left for the matinée, I installed our luggage at the Dorchester where we were to spend one night, then went to his last performance that evening, and we had supper at the Dorchester next to a table occupied by Jack Hulbert and Cicely Courtneidge. We were exhausted, excited and weak with happiness, and they gave us champagne and told us of their own wedding, which seemed to us to be a splendid omen of success. We tumbled into bed. Michael thought he was turning off the central heating, which he in fact jammed on, and we nearly died of heat.

The next night we spent in the sleeper going to Aberdeen and

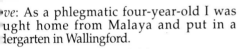

…ve: As a phlegmatic four-year-old I was …ught home from Malaya and put in a …dergarten in Wallingford.

…ve right: Though we children were never …n skiing lessons in Switzerland, my mother …lend me to some total strangers as ballast for …r boblet.

…w: My parents in an amateur production of … *Gondoliers* in Kuala Lumpur. Frustrated …rs often have professional actors as children.

…ow right: Schoolteacher in the jungle at …ser's Hill.

Above: In 1937 I enrolled at the Webber Douglas.
Michael Denison arrived in a bowler hat in my
second term.

Above: Despite my mother's opposition, we bec
officially engaged in March 1939.

Below: The white organdie dress, trimmed with
black, which I wore for our one-night honeymoon
at the Dorchester.

Below: The picture Michael took to war.

arrived at the station early next morning to find a huge placard with all our names on it and the words 'A. R. Whatmore's London Players. First time on any stage'. True about me but it didn't please the rest of the company.

Our leading man was Stewart Granger – already making a name for himself, handsome, self-confident and a good actor. His first words to me were, 'Do you lust after a sweet?' I thought this very racy and gratefully took one. His wife of nine months, Elspeth March, was beautiful (still is), and had a lovely speaking voice (she still has). She too was an excellent actress.

Stewart Granger's real name is James Stewart. He had had to change it as the Hollywood James Stewart was already famous. I, too, had to change my name from Bailey as there was another Dulcie Bailey on the stage, currently appearing in the West End in *The French for Love*. I found it hard to think of a good name. At one time I decided to call myself Angela Botibol – every tube station in London had an Angel Botibol tobacconist's kiosk and I thought at least the critics wouldn't for better or worse be able to overlook me. But I eventually took my mother's maiden name of Gray.

The opening play was *Hay Fever* by Noël Coward, and Michael and I were playing Simon and Sorel, the brother and sister, both very good parts. Wattie, as we all called A. R. Whatmore, was a splendid director. He was well known both in rep and in London, and enthusiastic and patient with me. He was always beautifully dressed, wore heavy hornrimmed spectacles and had a thin nasal voice. The cast were of a high standard, and the theatre, His Majesty's, is still our abiding favourite. The auditorium is still white and gold and red plush, and holds about one thousand seats: the perfect size. It was the cleanest theatre I have ever come across.

We had driven from the station to our digs through the 'granite city' in a very ancient Rolls, and this again seemed to us a good omen. In the squat grey house at 44 St Swithin's Street, we had a bedroom, a bathroom and a sitting-room, with a large breakfast, lunch, high tea and supper, at £2 each a week. As at Stansted, the food was very important to me. I was quite seriously undernourished by this time. Mrs Howe, our landlady, was plump and motherly. Mr Howe had been a sergeant in the Army. He had a red face, a straight back, a bristling moustache and a generous heart. There was also a terrier called Caesar who lived in the back yard. We took him out once but he was so frightened of the big wide world that he threw a fit.

Our employer was Peter Donald, one of four brothers who ran all the principal places of entertainment in Aberdeen, but it was Peter's idea to have straight drama instead of films at His Majesty's and from the start it paid off. He was wonderfully kind to us, lending us his 20 hp MG drop-head coupé with a tank full of petrol and a boot full of food and drink, when we were free (which was not often), and playing golf with Michael on the lovely seaside links of Balgownie. He is still a great friend.

On May 8th, 1939 the curtain rose on my first appearance and our first joint appearance. The house was full and I was very nervous. The scene opens with Sorel and Simon, two spoilt brats, lolling about on the stage and Sorel reading aloud from a book of advanced poetry – 'Love's a trollop stained with wine, Clawing at the breasts of adolescence.' At that moment the elastic of my pants broke. I had no idea what to do. The scene was a long one, with plenty of movement. I remembered vaguely that Mrs Patrick Campbell had once had the same trouble and that she had gone behind the sofa, dropped her pants and had then continued acting serenely, but in her day they wore long dresses. My dress came to the knee, but there was a sofa. With one hand clasped to my hips, I went behind the sofa. I was just about to wriggle the pants to the ground when I realised that this would be clearly seen by the people in the boxes, so resigned myself to keeping one hand or the other constantly on my hips. At the end of our duologue, we had to exit up the stairs. This was quite difficult as the pants were now around my knees. By bending in rather a curious fashion and moving fast, I managed it. The audience screamed with laughter, and I left to wild applause. It was a close-run thing but I had become a professional actress.

11

The Aberdeen season lasted until Saturday, September 2nd. In spite of the near certainty of a war, it had been a wonderfully happy time. We had been promised total annihilation almost at once by the press and wireless, so each and every day must be savoured. Living each day to its fullest potential is an exhilarating business, and we were very busy in the Whatmore company. Public response was entirely satisfactory, our parts varied and good, the notices excellent and Aberdeen and the countryside round it a glorious place for my first job. At that time I had no inkling of the humiliations, rejections and sheer bloody misery that would come along with the satisfactions and fulfilment of such a worthwhile career.

We rehearsed the play for the week after next in the morning, next week's in the afternoon, and played the current offering every evening except Sunday, and for two matinées. Living another person's life as vividly as one can is a very intense and interesting business and, at the beginning, one has to learn how to use one's hands and arms and voice, not only in the interests of character but also to appear natural. (Unfortunately I still walk badly.) Timing is all important and becomes partly instinct; a sense of humour is useful and a sense of comedy a necessity. A genuine sincerity and desire for truth is a great help. The charisma that makes a star was clearly visible in Stewart Granger even then, and also in Michael.

Half way through the season Jimmy had to leave for bigger things and, in August, Michael was summoned back to the Westminster for rehearsals of a new Priestley play *Music at Night*. He was to play the Communist poet – a most rewarding part. Elspeth and I soldiered on in Aberdeen.

Michael and I weren't parted for long. Every time Hitler made a particularly bellicose speech, rehearsals in London were called off and he took the night train to Aberdeen. When the tension seemed to ease, he went back to London. We had many many good friends in Scotland and, on the weekend war broke out, were staying at a tiny castle called

Mounie at Old Meldrum, just outside Aberdeen. The Setons were an enchanting family. On Sunday, September 3rd, we were all gathered in the small drawing-room in one of the castle turrets to hear Neville Chamberlain's speech on the radio. In a dry sad voice, he announced the outbreak of war. Immediately there was a flash of lightning, a clap of thunder and the phone went dead. Michael drove straight to Aberdeen to volunteer in the Gordon Highlanders. The Gordon Highlanders, like many a theatrical management in our careers, told him to go away. 'Don't call us. We'll call you.'

The Setons drove us to the town hall in Old Meldrum to collect their first evacuee children. All the big houses were to be used as billets for these poor little refugees. We sat and waited. After a short while one small Scots boy arrived. He had a gas mask in a cardboard case, a small cardboard suitcase, and he was dressed in his best clothes; all of which were too big for him, so that he could grow into them. He walked on to the lit dais and said bravely in a quavering voice, 'Wull, A'm heer' and was claimed by the woman who was to look after him. No other child came, so we all left.

Michael and I went down to London by train and saw our first barrage balloon sailing calmly in the autumn sunshine, a glinting silver elephant in the sky. We expected bombs daily. When they didn't materialise, the Government permitted the reopening of theatres, and *Music at Night* was the first straight play to open in wartime. Michael made a great personal success.

In the house we had rented in Draycott Avenue, I was having my first experience of domesticity and I hated it. I couldn't cook as indeed I had hardly ever been in a kitchen, so poor Michael had scrambled eggs, cheese and celery for weeks on end. I had bought a Mrs Beeton, unfortunately not up-dated, and for chicken soup she suggested 'Take twelve fowl and pluck them' (for haggis – 'Take the stomach bag of a sheep'!) which seemed too extravagant for our budget and too grisly for an amateur housewife. The Mask Theatre was a glorified rep so Michael spent the day rehearsing, then changed and gave a performance. He was up early to see to the very temperamental boiler in the basement, have breakfast and walk to work, and didn't return until about eleven p.m. for his supper. Having lived in crowds for as long as I could remember, I felt lonely for the first time in my life. The milkman, who was a jolly fellow, was the light of my life, and I bought everything at the Italian corner shop on a daily basis so that I could talk to someone.

Anne Somerset came to my rescue. She was already doing well and about to act in a company with Ivor Novello. Her father was entertainments officer at the RAF station at Grantham and wanted us to put on a show for him. We decided Sunday performances were possible and chose *Night Must Fall*, with Michael as Danny and me playing the Angela Baddeley part. We also played Portsmouth and Cranwell where, to our surprise, the bandmaster had composed very atmospheric incidental music for our performance. These activities were brought to a halt when we both became ill.

'What is the matter with me?' I asked.

The doctor, a large self-important red-faced man with a Sloane Street practice, gazed at me for a long time, then he said portentously, 'You have been married a year, I understand. That is the answer.'

'What is?' I asked in amazement.

'The first year of marriage,' he said solemnly.

'Good heavens!' I exclaimed. 'So what is the cure?'

'Marriage gets better as you go along.'

He was wrong in the diagnosis but right about the marriage.

I crossed Sloane Square in a daze, still feeling awful, and worried that marriage must have upset Michael badly too. On the way back home I passed Peter Jones and went up to the beauty department to have a facial. Moon-faced and very young, it was unlikely to achieve much, but I needed a psychological tonic. The beautician looked at me in surprise.

'Come to the window,' she said.

I obeyed.

'Show me your tongue.'

I did.

'Surely you have jaundice!' she said, and of course I had. So had Michael. We recovered together under the roof of kind friends. I still remember the luxury of a fire in our bedroom and watching the flames slowly dying in the dark at night, something I have longed to do ever since.

The Westminster season ended, Michael made his first film, *Tilly of Bloomsbury* with Michael Wilding, and then Wattie asked us to go back to Aberdeen. We were overjoyed. But at the same time Michael was asked by Binkie Beaumont, the biggest theatrical impresario of the time, to become a member of his HM Tennent repertory company to play in Edinburgh and Glasgow. The season was to open with *Music at Night*. It was clearly a big opportunity, but there was no job for me and, if Michael was to be called up, I must somehow keep the flag flying until his return. Would Wattie want me on my own?

In all the time we knew him, Binkie never changed; never seemed to grow any older. He was fair and very good-looking with large clear eyes and clipped speech. His skin was smooth, so was his persona. He was meticulously neat, a hard-headed businessman, but a loyal and considerate employer provided you delivered the goods. We both learned to love him. When Michael explained our situation, he sent for me and offered me the job of assistant stage manager. I refused.

'I'd be utterly incompetent!' I said, 'but I could play the juvenile in *Music at Night*.'

'What makes you think so, dear?' he asked dangerously.

'I've seen the play twenty-six times,' I said. 'I know it backwards. But we both love Aberdeen and Wattie, and you're offering me no more money.'

'A pound more,' he said, 'and you are on trial.'

So I was engaged and we joined his company.

The company, led by Mary Jerrold and Marjorie Fielding, was prestigious, the plays good and we all got on very well as a team, which also included Cyril Cusack, Clive Morton, Rosalie Crutchley and Sonia Dresdel. No-one treated me as a beginner and Michael and I were again given excellent parts. We did a weekly shuttle service between Edinburgh and Glasgow, half the company opening simultaneously in each city with different plays, and exchanging for the second week of the run. Esmé Church and Murray MacDonald, who became a good friend and for whom we often worked later, were the directors.

Then suddenly the Battle of France was in progress and soon the Battle of Britain. Michael was called up in mid-June to the Royal Signals. On the Monday he and I were acting together, on Tuesday after watching Alan MacNaughtan, his successor, and me in *The Last of Mrs Cheyney* from the back of the circle, he slipped away through the blackout to Waverley Station, to join his draft en route for Whitby, which they reached at seven a.m. next morning. They then walked (no-one could yet march properly) up a hill to breakfast and then to a row of empty redbrick boarding houses which they occupied, sitting on the floor, six to a room. By late morning, those of them who had ever fired a rifle – almost none – were in slit trenches with five rounds of ammunition each, as the front-line defence of Whitby. Luckily Hitler didn't think of invading Britain via Whitby that June!

Michael's squad consisted of twenty-three Glasgow Post Office workers and himself. No-one could understand Michael's English accent and he couldn't understand them, but with the help of Bobby Melvin, the squad comedian, who laughed hysterically but not unkindly at everything Michael said, he was treated as the squad mascot rather than as an outsider. Their pay was 15/- a week, half of which was automatically deducted from married men. After a fortnight, real soldiers were found to defend Whitby. Until his death Bobby Melvin was a friend.

Meanwhile on the night Michael left the Tennent Players Edinburgh had its first air raid. Ada Reeve, a great old musical comedy actress, was also in my digs and Ada, with a pile of her best hats beside her, lay face downwards in the corridor chewing cotton wool to lessen the blast. She commanded me to do the same.

Binkie came up to Edinburgh to tell the company that with business falling owing to the war, the season could only continue if the company would take salary cuts. He then came into my dressing-room and told me that everyone had agreed that Michael's departure for the Army was cut enough for me. I have never stopped being grateful for his kindness. A young up-and-coming writer, fair-haired with glasses and very pink cheeks called Alan Melville, then with the BBC Scottish service, also came to see me to say that if he was ever in a position to give me a job, he would do so. He was, and he did within a few months.

The season came to an end and, shortly afterwards, through the good offices of Sonia Dresdel, I was given a job at Harrogate with the White Rose Players. This meant I was within reach of Michael who was now a lance-corporal at Ossett, near Huddersfield.

Harrogate had been almost free from bombs and one would hardly have known there was a war on except for the newspapers. I actually saw the only two bombs falling. I was shopping and suddenly heard the drone of an aeroplane. Sure that it was 'one of ours' I waved to the pilot, whom I could clearly see, and only then noticed the black cross painted on the plane. As the bombs hurtled down I and another woman knelt hurriedly in a small area entirely surrounded by glass. One bomb fell on the Majestic Hotel. It didn't explode but frightened a chambermaid who found she was being chased down the passage by a huge 'bouncing ball' as she described it. The theory in those days was that it must have been made by the Czechs who hated the Germans and so made duds. The other fell fairly near us but, apart from blowing out the glass all round us, it did the other woman and me no harm at all.

Although Michael and I could now see quite a lot of one another, I found the company an unhappy one. It was run by two women, a mother and daughter called Mrs Peacock and Marie Blanche. Both had once been well known on the stage and they were very jealous of the young girls. The young Trevor Howard, fresh from his success in London in *French Without Tears*, was there and we became good friends. He was ruggedly handsome with a slow charming smile, and much in love with a pretty blonde, not in the company, called Mavis Labatouche, so we had one of those rare male-female friendships uncomplicated by sex and, after spending all week together, went our separate ways at the weekend. My life *was* complicated however by the fact that Sonia, unbeknown to me, had had an affair with the unbelievably boring director, and he regarded me as a stand-in. He pinched my behind every time I passed his office on the turn of the dressing-room stairs. One day I could bear it no longer and said with icy politeness, 'I wonder if you could vary your pinching routine. It is not so much the fact that my behind is black and blue as that the monotony is getting me down.' The small flame of lust that he had for me died an immediate death, and an energetic and bitter hatred took its place. My days at Harrogate were numbered and, when my female employers insisted on me wearing an exceptionally badly made outsize blonde wig because there were two brunettes and a redhead, but no daffodil blonde in the company, I gave in my notice and returned to London.

12

Almost at once I was offered the chance to do six episodes for a radio serial to be called *Front Line Family*, written by our new Scottish friend Alan Melville. This I accepted gratefully, if mildly guiltily, as Michael and I had recently got ourselves an agent and I was rather embarrassed at the fact that I had found the radio work by myself. I needn't have been.

Back in London I went to call on Binkie who had been so kind to me, glad that I didn't look as if I were asking for work. As soon as he saw me Binkie drawled, 'Well, well, dear! We are grand, aren't we, to refuse such a lovely tour! And not even to bother to ring me up yourself, either.'

Bewildered, I asked him what he meant and he told me that our new agency had turned down an offer for me to play the juvenile in a tour with A.E. Matthews and Marie Tempest.

'But they never even told me about it!' I exclaimed.

'Sack them!' said Binkie, and I did.

So I lost the tour with Marie Tempest and A. E. Matthews, but heard that she had been very bad-tempered throughout, as Binkie wasn't going to bring the play into London because he didn't want her exposed to the air raids. Apparently even going up to his office in the Globe Theatre in the tiny lift which could only just hold two people jammed together, she had been cross. Mattie had said 'Good morning Mary' on seeing her and had raised his hat and kissed her on her cheek. She didn't answer. He tried a few more pleasantries which she totally ignored, so he remained silent and put his hat back on. When they reached their destination Mattie opened the lift gates, swept off his hat, got out of the lift, bowed ceremoniously and said, 'After such proximity, Mary, I can only offer you marriage.'

Front Line Family was a BBC propaganda serial designed to bring America into the war by showing the courage and humour of an ordinary British family undaunted by Hitler. It was to run five days a week for six weeks. When I left it after a year, it was still running and, after the war, the name was changed to *The Robinson Family*. It was Britain's first soap opera. The Robinsons were played by Nell Ballantyne, an old friend of Alan's, and Ernest Butcher, a well-known variety artist. Their son was Tony Halfpenny, Nancy Nevinson was the daughter and I the daughter-in-law. Lovely Gladys Spencer (still acting at ninety-five) was the family friend. The Blitz was on. London was sandbagged and trenched; soldiers, sailors and airmen, ATS, Wrens and WAAFs were everywhere and we broadcast at first from Broadcasting House in Portland Place and then at Maida Vale.

Alan, Nell and I shared a flat in Maida Vale. I was given the only double room to accommodate Michael when he came on leave. Each time he did, by an extraordinary coincidence, the bombing stopped and Alan wrote him into the script. It was an amusing and steady job. We all became friends and the broadcasts were heard all over the world – even by my family in Singapore.

One day Alan asked me to read a revue of his called *Sweet and Low* to see if it was funny. Not only I thought it funny. With its successors *Sweeter and Lower* and *Sweetest and Lowest* it was to run in the West End for several years with Hermione Gingold and Hermione Baddeley.

Late in 1941 came the Japanese invasion of Malaya. Mummy, Rosamund and Roger were all there. Mummy's letters radiated confidence in the impregnability of Singapore until almost the very end. Roger joined the Malay States Volunteers and was imprisoned in Changi, though we had no news of this until 1945. Rosamund managed to escape with her husband to Australia, sending a cable simply saying 'Safe. Rosamund.' But whether it was only she – she and her husband or the whole family – I didn't know. Finally Mummy fled to Java from where she took a small Dutch steamer called the *Roosboom* to bring her to England. In the Indian Ocean the ship was bombed by the Japanese and sunk. There were very few survivors and Mummy was not among them.

Even now I can hardly bear to think of it. She was only in her fifties and had such courage and vitality. I only hope the bomb killed her at once and she wasn't left to drown or starve in a lifeboat.

I didn't hear about any of this for several months.

Here is one of the entries from her diary at the time, strangely discovered by Brian Montgomery, the brother of the Field Marshal, who quoted it in his book *Shenton of Singapore* about Sir Shenton Thomas, the last Governor before the fall of Malaya.

Sunday January 25th, 1942. More and more troops and equipment are pouring into the island, and soon with any luck, we shall have enough men, planes and tanks to turn the Japs out. We are not out of the woods yet and must not relax for a second, but it is a wonderful comfort to us all to know that these necessary fighting forces are on their way. Spent the day as usual at the [Tanglin] Club where I was able to entertain some up-country people – if it were not for the unhappy cause of their being in Singapore, it would be all the more delightful.

Monday January 26th. It was extraordinary how many more work people were moving about today; they had been frightened by the Japanese broadcasts about flattening the city on Sunday. The clerks were all smiling when I got down [to the Raffles Library] and their reaction to the whole thing is better.

What a mess that whole campaign was! Absolutely no air cover for the two great battleships the *Repulse* and the *Prince of Wales*, which were therefore sunk at once. No proper air cover for the rest of the island either and a civilian population kept in total ignorance. We betrayed Malaya by not having the ability to defend her properly, and disillusioned her people by offering means of escape to British women and children, but none to theirs. Many of the carefree young men who holidayed up the Hill were killed on the Burma railway. Many many others, and my girlfriends too, were imprisoned and tortured in the camps. Even now, fifty years later, some of these suffer from terrible nightmares and depressions. My brother who was a prisoner in Changi is one, but at least he has a family who understands what he has been through.

Not knowing any of this, I had an extraordinary encounter with the BBC Far Eastern Service who asked me to meet one of their members at the Criterion Theatre. I did and first of all was asked to sing 'I don't want to set the world on fire' with Mantovani and his orchestra, and then to compose and sing a song about Singapore. Word had apparently reached them that I had lived in Malaya – but surely not of my early attempts at writing hit songs! I did this too (the song was called simply 'Singapore') and, with the actor Hugh Burden as accompanist on the piano, I broadcast it to be relayed to Malaya. It was a great success in Singapore and was broadcast no less than fourteen times. I wonder if poor Mummy ever heard it?

After a year with *Front Line Family*, I had a summons from Robert

Atkins for an audition to play Shakespeare in various parks in England for the 'Stay at home for your holidays scheme'. My parts were to be Maria in *Twelfth Night*, Hermia in *A Midsummer Night's Dream* and Bianca in *The Taming of the Shrew*. It was an extraordinary engagement, but then Robert was an extraordinary man. We opened for a week at Platt Fields in Manchester, spent several days at The Boggart Hole Clough, known locally as T' Boggart Ole, and then slowly zigzagged down to Regent's Park. At the Boggart Hole which we reached from our digs in the city by tram, we acted one day in the pouring rain to an audience composed entirely of Indians huddled in mackintoshes under umbrellas. The performance was broadcast. Robert hadn't told us we were on the air because the fee was too small in his opinion to be divided. Helen Cherry, a beautiful redhead of twenty-one who later married Trevor Howard, was playing Hippolyta, and started off by tripping and falling flat across the microphones; Mary Martlew, playing Helena, tangled up the line 'Never did mockers waste more idle breath,' saying simply 'Never did wockers' and collapsing with laughter, and I who had never understood the line 'Emptying their bosoms of their counsels sweet' tried the line out anxiously in several versions, thereby corpsing the entire cast. One of the most important of the small part players, who preferred sleeping with Canadian soldiers to acting, was missing throughout.

It was sad that Robert never got a knighthood. He wanted one so badly; he was passionately patriotic and passionately loyal to the crown. Both even took precedence over his passion for Shakespeare. He was tubby, white-faced, bald except for a tonsure of white hair and he waved his pudgy hands constantly as he spoke. It was Robert who kept Shakespeare alive for many years in this country, and he had to scrape the money together, always needing more but always doing wonders on a shoestring. If anyone deserved an honour, he did. The stories about him are legion and, without the mimicry of his plummy voice, they lose some of their humour, but I will attempt two.

After rehearsals, Robert, like every other director, gave notes. He was star struck and always called out the names of the senior members of a company first. Once, however, tense with rage, he called out a young man whose only job had been to hold a spear throughout the play. This he had done with drooping elegance. Robert waved at him imperiously. Astonished, the young man came forward. Robert addressed him solemnly, shaking with anger.

'I don't like your conception, old man,' he said. 'It's unsoldierly, inaccurate and arouses the gravest suspicions, old man.'

Another time, when he was running Stratford, he was most indignant to find that all the leading ladies of his company had been asked to read the lessons in church but no-one had yet asked him. He stormed in to see the clergyman and, jutting out his chin at him, said,

'Can you give me one cogent reason why I shouldn't read the f-----g lesson?'

I love the use of the word cogent!

At last we opened with *Twelfth Night* in Regent's Park. It had rained all the tour, our velvet dresses had been soaking wet for weeks but miraculously they came back from the cleaners almost as good as new.

The Open Air Theatre then had a long narrow stage of grass, about thirty or forty yards wide, with deckchairs facing it up a slope. We dressed in two tents behind a hedge of privet and syringa. A third tent had a wooden stage and wooden chairs and acted as a secondary theatre if the weather made things impossible outside.

At one matinée of *A Midsummer Night's Dream*, the young man playing Philostrate became totally disillusioned with his part. Although Philostrate is a very small part, he had apparently expected good reviews. When those were not forthcoming, he decided to draw attention to himself. If it was really pouring so hard that even a long-suffering British audience wanted no more, someone from the company was deputed, at a suitable moment, to say that the play would continue in the tent. On this particular blazing summer day this young man suddenly interrupted the show by handing his scroll to Theseus and loudly announcing 'Ladies and gentlemen, owing to the inclemency of the weather, we shall all now proceed into the tent.' In spite of the sunshine, the obedient audience filed into the small, stuffy tent and we had to follow them to finish the performance.

Our first performance was a matinée and, in spite of having a good deal against us, though not that day the weather, we had good notices. My personal notices interested Binkie enough for him to send Kitty Black as a talent scout to see me and she reported so favourably that I was sent for the audition for Alexandra, the girl of fifteen in *The Little Foxes* which was to be put on at the Piccadilly Theatre with Fay Compton in the lead and the nineteen-year-old Richard Attenborough in the cast.

My audition took place on the stage of the Piccadilly Theatre with Emlyn Williams, who was going to direct, playing my mother and the only audience, Binkie, in the stalls. They both liked my performance and we all three went back to Binkie's office in the Globe to discuss finances, rehearsal schedules and so on. As I was leaving the office, on air with excitement, Emlyn said kindly, 'Won't your Mummy and Daddy be pleased?'

'They are both dead,' I replied, 'but I'll tell my husband and he'll be delighted.'

'Your husband?' asked Emlyn in amazement.

His face fell. Married women shouldn't be playing fifteen-year-olds, and the next day I was told I had lost the job.

Auditions went on for the part, then a week later the telephone rang.

'Come this afternoon for another interview,' said Kitty. 'Wear bows *everywhere*. They still think you gave the best audition but Emlyn is worried about your age.'

Nervously I ascended in the Globe's tiny lift and, to my horror, I was in it with my double. We smiled at each other, I anxiously, she serenely. When we reached the office, the other girl was shown straight in and I was left to wait on the sofa. I waited a long time and she came back smiling broadly and disappeared. I went for the interview and it was successful. The bows and a pink candy-striped frock had evidently won. Kitty was as excited as I was.

'But what about the other girl?' I asked.

'What other girl?' asked Kitty.

'The one who came with me,' I said.

'There wasn't another girl,' she said.

'But I saw her,' I objected. 'We came up in the lift together.'

'There was no-one,' she returned.

'She has only just gone out,' I said.

'Oh her!' exclaimed Kitty. 'She wasn't an actress. She came about some costume hire!'

So at last, three and a half years after leaving the Webber Douglas, I was on my way to becoming a West End actress and, in those days, the West End was the Mecca of all actors.

13

The war! Some people have a nostalgia for it, I have none. I am a terrible coward but strangely was hardly ever frightened then, although like everyone else I was in a state of wary apprehension. The horrors and the heroism, the stoicism, the great set pieces of Dunkirk, the Battle of Britain, the Desert War, and war in Malaysia and the Far East were part of daily living, as were the fact that Michael was away, Mummy, Roger and Rosamund were still in Singapore, and all one's friends everywhere were coping with tragedies and tedium in about equal measure. There were also the inconveniences. The clothes rationing didn't worry me; I had seldom had many clothes and I discovered hats, which transformed everything – and me. They suit me. Food rationing I was used to. Being without Michael was a constant bereavement but I worked hard, as I have always had to do, and enjoyed my work tremendously.

London was both grim and gay. The blackout, the sandbags, the sirens, the tired faces of everyone, the awful results of the bombing and the smell from the bombed houses, the smoke, the snaking fire-hoses, the hooch instead of drink, the American soldiers, the jitterbug, the RAF boys with their handlebar moustaches, absurd voices and magnificent bravery, the constant presence of death and the constant reaction of humour to make it tolerable, the emergence of women as partners in the defence of Britain, and the overall grime, are unforgettable. Also my feeling of being in two places at once; London where I was becoming a big star and Malaya where the bottom had fallen out of the world.

The London theatres were packed solid; mostly light comedy was on offer. Neither the audience nor the actors paid the slightest overt attention to the bombs, but everyone was acutely aware of them. The sets and costumes showed no signs of austerity – after all, plays were kept running to keep up the spirits of the people – but the Queens Theatre in Shaftesbury Avenue was destroyed entirely by a bomb, and the Phoenix had a near miss. Peggy Ashcroft was hit by a V2 bomb during rehearsals and blown straight into a barber's shop. She got glass in her knee which has troubled her ever since. In the theatre as elsewhere both actors and public were astonishingly brave.

But not everywhere was sweetness and light. A beautiful young cousin of mine had her leg blown off during the raid on the Café de Paris. The doctor attending to the wounded had everything stolen from his pockets. The ladies' cloakroom was looted and my cousin, lying on the pavement waiting for the ambulance with her furs over her to keep her warm, had them stolen off her.

Michael was moved from Ossett to Halifax, from Halifax to Cornwall and from Cornwall to the Officer Cadet Training Unit at Bulford, becoming in due course a second-lieutenant in the Intelligence Corps. He had left me to become a soldier, a romantic-looking young actor with longish and luxuriant brown hair. The first time I saw him again as a signaller he was close-cropped in an ill-fitting khaki uniform and I didn't recognise him. On most of his leaves we tried to spend one evening dining and dancing at the Savoy. Carroll Gibbons was the band-leader and no-one in the services who went to the Savoy at that time, or their dancing partners, will forget him. He was the acceptable face of war. Like every entertainer in every theatre, he carried on playing even in the worst air raids.

My West End début was prestigious but short-lived. For the entire three weeks of its run, *The Little Foxes* was plagued by thick impenetrable fog. At the dress rehearsal, even the auditorium was filled with fog – but also with the entire theatrical profession. Edith Evans was in front and sent me messages of encouragement, although she had never met me, and Vivien Leigh, remembering that I was Michael's wife, sent me a ravishing little bouquet of roses in a pottery vase which is in front of me now. I don't, I'm afraid, remember what the notices were like for the production. For me they were excellent and I heard the first faint murmurs of real personal success. I had had intimations in my previous jobs, but this was 'the big time', as someone described it to me.

We came off, however, and Emlyn asked me to stay with him for Christmas near Didcot in Berkshire, as Michael was away. Emlyn was one of the wittiest men I have ever met and as kind as he was witty. Brilliantly gifted, he had a mind like quicksilver and a wary and diagonal approach to life. Very Welsh, generally optimistic but with a strain of deep pessimism, he was small, wiry, dark and good-looking. Molly his wife, and Alan and Brooke his two sons, were there. Alan

ove: My first star billing, as the Cockney waitress Rose, with Dickie Attenborough in the stage version of *ghton Rock*. It brought me a contract with Gainsborough Pictures and fanmail from Aleister Crowley.
ow: Right, the publicity picture that Gainsborough plastered on all the buses, and left, how they cast me
my second film, *A Place of One's Own*.

Above: Left, on location in Italy with Kieron Moore in *A Man About the House*; despite rave notices for *The* *Were Sisters* with James Mason, right, Gainsborough sacked me.

Below: Michael returned to post-war acting in the title role in *My Brother Jonathan*. It was the first film i which we acted together.

and Brooke by coincidence were at my old school, St Anthony's, Wallingford, where my Auntie D was now teaching. She heard that I had been staying with them and asked them how they had liked me.

'But we had no-one at all to stay,' they said. I don't know if that was a compliment or a criticism!

I was asked to audition for the part of the Cockney waitress, Rose, in the stage version of Graham Greene's *Brighton Rock*, in which Dickie Attenborough was to play Pinkie, and Hermione Baddeley was the star. The auditions were to last a week. Dickie told me to take my shoes off because he was very short (but very attractive in those days with his large eyes, snub nose and sensual mouth) and to look as pathetic as I could. What effect this advice had, I don't know, but I got the part, and a few weeks later, with Michael over from Belfast in front, the play opened to critical acclaim. The next morning my name was put above the title which, in theatrical billing parlance, meant I had become a star. It couldn't of course be put up in lights. There weren't those sort of lights in the blackout. I had a new agent, Jack Dunfee, and a contract with Gainsborough Films. Also the next morning Michael, who had come over with an inflamed and septic leg as a result of a football injury, had a high temperature and had to go on M & B, the new wonder drug. Our tiny flat in Dolphin Square was filled with flowers, photographers, journalists and the district nurse who had been brought in to look after Michael. She hated the lot of us.

Aleister Crowley, who was a well-known diabolist, sent me a privately printed pamphlet called *The Fun of the Fair* (copy 176). In the back of it he wrote:

> If you should go to Brighton Rock
> Prepare yourself against a shock
> It isn't that she's playing Baddeley
> But in this world things turn out madly:-
> A young thing stole the show away,
> Her dulcet name is Dulcie Gray.

He signed it with his name followed by the words 'with sincere homage and every good wish'.

I sent a letter of thanks, and he then sent me a letter suggesting that I be sacrificed as a virgin (I was again playing a sixteen-year-old) at dawn in a midsummer rite at Stonehenge.

I asked our agent, Jack Dunfee, what I should do and he told me to send a letter back saying that I disliked getting up early. I heard no more from Mr Crowley.

Working with Totie, as Hermione Baddeley was always called, was an astonishing experience. Parties erupted all round her all day and all night. She hated being alone for a moment, had a host of friends and unending energy. She also had a very old cocker spaniel called Mr Bags. His black coat had a curious green sheen and, when Totie and I had to share a bedroom in the various digs and hotels in which we stayed on the pre-London run (everywhere was bursting with servicemen on leave), he preferred my bed to hers, and he stank to high heaven. He had also perfected a way of travelling free by train. When he heard the ticket collector he would hide under the seat until the man had gone and, when we reached our destination, he hopped out of the carriage and trotted down the platform waving his tail and obviously looking for someone. At the far side of the exit gate, he waited for Totie.

With total generosity in all things, she was a stimulating companion. She seemed happy always but she never ceased to mourn the end of her first marriage. I don't know whether 'Dozie' Willis was her second husband or her third. He was a strange man. He had served with some gallantry as a soldier in India and stood very upright. He seemed totally absent-minded and spoke monosyllabically through such clenched teeth that it was almost impossible to understand a word. If you could make out even a banal sentence like 'It's a fine day' you felt as if you had been given a present. Although they were utterly unalike, they seemed to get on well. He was shy and withdrawn and not very social. She embraced everyone and every situation with enormous enthusiasm. There is a story about them which used to go the rounds and illustrates this disparity but which is, I'm sure, apocryphal. It is said they were staying at the Welsh Pony in Oxford where Totie found a very attractive young man at the bar. The story goes that he asked her to sleep with him and she took him up to her room – quite forgetting that this time she was there with Dozie. When both were completely undressed and preparing to get into bed, the door opened and Dozie came in.

'Dozie Willis, by all that's holy!' said the young man joyfully.

'Good God! Haven't seen you since Waziristan!' exclaimed Dozie, showing no surprise that a stranger was in the marital bedroom and that both the young man and his wife were stark naked. The two men talked about India and the Army until the small hours, while a very cross Totie got into bed by herself.

She was a brilliant actress and her performance in *Brighton Rock* was magnificent. It was she who introduced me to Viva King and her soirées in Thurloe Square where I met Norman Douglas, large, big-boned and very white, Nina Hamnett the artist and sculptress (nearly always drunk), Esmé Percy, a famous if eccentric little actor with one unwinking glass eye, and Osbert Lancaster. Osbert Lancaster once told me that he perfectly remembered being taken out in his pram as a baby and the delicious sense of power it gave him to throw his toys on the ground, knowing that they would be picked up and returned. Viva was extremely knowledgeable about antique glass among other things; and her husband, who looked like a boiled lobster and was a noted Far-Eastern linguist, hovered vaguely around us. They were happy and instructive afternoons.

Totie also introduced me to three wonderful taxi drivers, Bert and Arthur Jenkins, and Little Joe Ambridge. They were passionately interested in the theatre and quite miraculously kind to me. Any time there was a bad blitz, one of them came to the theatre to take me home, whether I could afford it or not. Sometimes they even came with passengers who had no desire to go to Pimlico! If I could pay I did. If I couldn't, I gave them tea in my flat. There was only one difficulty. Bert and Arthur couldn't get round the name Dulcie. Bert called me Duliss, and Arthur called me Ducille. When Michael was there calling me Dulcie, the conversation sounded like the Mad Hatter's Tea Party. One day after the show, when I was going to a late-night party at Viva's, I asked if Bert could join us as it was late and he was very tired. She agreed, and he kept us all enthralled. He unexpectedly knew a great deal about glass and he had been Lawrence of Arabia's batman.

The theatre then was a family affair. The great meeting place was the Ivy Restaurant after the show. Tables near the door were reserved for theatre 'Royalty' – Noël Coward, Ivor Novello, Laurence Olivier, Vivien Leigh, Kay Hammond and, of course, Totie and many more. Small fry sat at the back of the restaurant, but had to run the gauntlet of the great stars. If you had made it, everyone seemed genuinely delighted, although repartee was quick and not always kind. Lilian Braithwaite, an old actress of extreme grace, had a kind heart but a very sharp tongue. For some reason she had taken against Sonia Dresdel and, when Ivor came up to her table leading Sonia by the hand saying enthusiastically 'My dear, would you like to meet Sonia Dresdel?' she answered firmly, 'No thank you dear,' and went on eating. Ivor also gave her and Fay Compton diamond brooches and she thought that hers was smaller than Fay's so, seeing Fay and Ivor together one evening, she went up to them and said sweetly to Fay, 'Fay darling, what a lovely brooch Ivor has given you! Can you *see* mine?' If this makes her sound a bitch, she wasn't. In a good mood she was dazzling and enchanting.

Years later, when I was starring in the film *A Man About the House*, she had a bit part. Although at that time she was also starring in the evenings in *Arsenic and Old Lace* at the Duchess Theatre, she wasn't given a chair to sit in. I privately had my name taken off mine and had hers put on. She gave no sign that she had noticed but, after the film was over, an enormous bouquet of flowers arrived for me and the note read, 'I saw what you did my dear. With love from an Autumn actress to a Spring one. Lilian.'

Some time in 1942 I was asked to test for a leading part in the film of Ben Travers' *Banana Ridge* set in Malaya, to be made with Isobel Jeans, Alfred Drayton and Robertson Hare, at Welwyn Garden City for ABC. Michael had a sudden weekend leave and I offered to cancel my test. But he was hating being away from the theatre for so long and said he'd rather come with me, so we went together. The scene was a love scene and the lover was the camera with a young man beside it to read the lines. He wasn't a professional and read badly, so I asked if I could act with Michael. Michael was allowed to do the scene and the other five girls also testing asked to borrow him too. In all he made six tests. None of us got the girl's part. Michael couldn't get his as he was in the Army.

I was then given a test on my own and told by a sympathetic camera man that Nova Pilbeam had already been chosen, so there was no film in the camera. Furious, I went to see Walter Mycroft, the head of the studios. He was a dwarf but sitting down looked most impressive. Apparently touched by my outburst, he gave me the tiny part of a secretary and, on hearing that I came from Malaya, the job of 'Malayan technical advisor' to the film. It carried the pay of £5 a week and the perk of first-class railway travel.

To do the film I had to travel from Dolphin Square by the workmen's tram at four a.m., then take a train to the studios at Welwyn. At the beginning of the film I was also acting in *Brighton Rock* in London and so didn't get home until about eleven p.m. when

I cleaned the flat and had three hours' sleep. I remember distinctly that at this point I decided that I had been young for too long! The play over, Robert Newton, a great actor but an alcoholic, weaved his way on to our set one day. He invited me to a drink which I could resist, but a lift home, which I couldn't, and after filming was over we both went to the pub next door. He became involved in a fierce argument with another customer and eventually swapped his car for a horse. He offered me a ride, but I luckily refused as he wasn't seen again for three days.

The run of *Brighton Rock* finished and Dickie Attenborough was called up. Michael was given an overseas posting, which turned out to be Egypt. His embarkation leave fitted neatly into the space between *Brighton Rock* and my next job, *Landslide*.

Life without him at home was bleak, but I looked forward to *Landslide* because it was to be directed by John Gielgud. Unfortunately it didn't work as a play and John could make nothing of it. He was a worrying director for me at this time, as his modesty made him ask advice from anyone around and he frequently changed his mind. He is now a friend and a man whom I wholeheartedly admire. Sad, sad, sad for me, that this was my only professional meeting with him. He is renowned for his social clangers but, though still immensely shy, he is a very amusing and witty talker. He was beautiful to look at in youth. In old age, on the tips of his toes, speaking so quickly that it is sometimes hard to understand him, he is beautiful too. His face radiates humour, curiosity, intelligence and kindness. He is loved and respected by the entire profession.

Now I began filming again. My first part under my contract with Gainsborough was a tiny one – a girl in an internment camp in France, carrying a bucket about, in a film called *2000 Women* at Lime Grove Studios. Next came the heroine's friend in a weepy with Phyllis Calvert and Stewart Granger called *Madonna of the Seven Moons*.

The studios are now very shabby and used by the BBC, but even then they were pretty ramshackle. They were run by two Polish brothers, Maurice and Isidore Ostrer. We contract artists each had a private dressing-room. Mine was a cell but at least the lift man, Harry, wore a rose in his buttonhole every day. The passage to the offices of the Ostrers and the other producers and directors was known as the Polish Corridor and was always in a turmoil of intrigue. Gainsborough, with Maurice at the helm, made some of the most successful British films ever. *The Wicked Lady* starring Margaret Lockwood, James

Mason and Stewart Granger, and *The Man in Grey* with the same trio and Phyllis Calvert, had broken all records; but now everyone in the place seemed to be battling for power and soon the company was to be sold to Rank in a state of near collapse.

R. J. Minney, one of the producers, was immediately friendly and showed me round on the first day, and also into a strange little no-man's-land of a room which he called the Green Room. 'You'll be using this,' he said cheerfully, and I gathered that my theatrical (as opposed to film) roots had been noted.

The stars who, as well as those already named, included Anne Crawford, Patricia Roc, Jean Kent, Michael Rennie, Eric Portman and eventually myself, had our lunch at the 'Stars' table' in the general canteen, but we were waited on instead of having to help ourselves. The Brothers and the other VIPs had their meal in a room to themselves next door.

Anne Crawford and I became fast friends. She was already suffering from the leukaemia that killed her in her thirties, but one would never have known it. She was a beautiful fair-haired Scots girl, always laughing in spite of the fact that she was both ill and going through an unhappy love affair, and we spent a good deal of our free time together. Maggie Lockwood, the top film star of her day, was utterly unconceited, down to earth and professional – a lovely girl with a Rabelaisian laugh. When she heard that I didn't go down to the shelters under Dolphin Square during the raids because our flat was so small and on the fifth floor and had three floors above, so that I felt safe, she said, 'But there must be windows in your bedroom. What about flying glass? You could damage your face and finish your career.' So I slept in the bathroom which had no windows. Maggie loved Bert's name for me of Duliss and always called me that.

It is odd that such a nostalgic glow now bathes the films of the 'forties and 'fifties, because the Gainsborough films at least were then despised by the intelligentsia and most of the critics. Immensely popular with the public, they suffered the fate that most very successful middle-brow films, television plays and series suffer in this country, ridicule and scorn. James Mason, the most popular male star of the time, told me he would never get good notices for his acting unless he went to America, where he would cease to be only a successful British actor, and become an international star whom press barbs would no longer be able to affect. I made my first starring picture *They Were Sisters* with James, and I was in Manchester when it was being shown there. I was trying to buy a reel of cotton. The shop assistant recognised me.

'Oh, you *aren't* Dulcie Gray, are you?'

'Yes.'

'And you were hit by James Mason in the film?'

'Yes.'

She fainted with excitement!

During the war we also made propaganda films. I did two. One was a totally unmemorable film for the Soldiers, Sailors and Air Force Fund. This, like many of the propaganda films, was crude and almost childish. The other was a Savings Short with John Mills, aimed to make people save money for the war effort. It is a collector's piece as it was directed by Jessie Matthews. Although Jessie was probably our greatest musical comedy film star ever, she couldn't direct and she insisted on showing Johnnie, already an established and much loved star, how to act and in particular how to do his love scenes with me. It was hilarious but not comfortable.

In 1944 I had my first experience of touring in Europe for the troops with ENSA (Entertainment National Service Association). We went in uniform so that if captured we would be treated as prisoners of war and not shot as spies. The play was *Lady from Edinburgh* and our pre-West End tour was Lille, Amiens, Dieppe, Eindhoven, Ghent, Brussels, Bruges, Paris, Versailles, Inverness, Cardiff and then the Playhouse, London.

France, Holland and Belgium had just been liberated but they were all reeling from four years of occupation, and everywhere there were shortages and a feeling of exhausted relief rather than exhilaration. Paris was particularly crushed and grim. Most of the women wore shovel hats, padded shoulders on short black frocks, and clogs. In Lille I asked the name of a tailor as my uniform didn't fit anywhere, and was directed to a small huddle of houses on the outskirts of the town. Here the tailor, his wife and neighbours had been trying to exist on a huge communal pan of soup for months, and the tailor's wife was very sick. I luckily knew someone from the Catering Corps in the town and managed to get a large sack of food for them. The tailor refused to take it because he was too proud to accept charity. He wept – I wept too, and told him that as Christmas was near and I was away from my family, I wanted to give him and his wife a present. Finally he accepted, and I have always hoped his wife recovered.

In Eindhoven where we were playing at the Phillips factory theatre, we had a very curious time. On New Year's Day, a brilliantly sunny day with snow on the ground, I was looking out of the window and saw an enchantingly pretty scene. Silver parachutes were floating gently down in the still air and from the ground came little puffs of white smoke. It was in fact a determined attack by the Luftwaffe on Eindhoven, which was Monty's Headquarters, and the parachutists were presumably German aircrew baling out. Perhaps because of this we were kept a week longer than planned in Eindhoven and, at the hairdresser's one day wearing a scarf and earrings to cheer up the drab khaki of my uniform, I was hurriedly smuggled out of the back door, 'because some Germans were coming in at the front'. One night when we were going to a party, the passengers in the taxi behind were shot. For the local people, as for us, they were uncertain, dangerous days.

The Marie Antoinette Theatre in Versailles was exquisite (though the lavatories were foul), and Alan Melville was in the audience. At Inverness I went to my first auction sale at Fraser's antique shop, meaning to get a vase or a small trinket to celebrate the fifth anniversary of our engagement. I bought a fourposter bed, two Queen Anne tables, a small satinwood table, a sofa, a marquetry settee and two chairs, and a Meissen coffee service for £80 the lot. I had spent our entire savings! The furniture from Michael's old home had been destroyed in the Blitz, so if we ever achieved a home of our own we should indeed need furniture, but on the other hand what on earth would Michael say? Horrified and delighted simultaneously at my spending spree, I asked when the goods could be sent. 'In wartime with the petrol situation, not for some months,' said the salesman. This was a relief as there certainly wouldn't be any room in the flat in Dolphin Square.

In Cardiff the landlady asked sternly, 'Do you drink?'

'I do, but I don't get drunk if I can help it,' I replied.

'Then you can't come here,' she said. 'I don't have anyone drinking here. Dainty Dolly died of drink last week. 4711 Eau de Cologne.'

We opened in London to good notices and the play ran three years, although I left it after one.

Michael meanwhile had been sent from Egypt to Greece, as a member of the liberating forces. They were greeted with flowers and kisses, and Michael's unit was billeted in the once smart suburb of Kifisia. Six weeks later, tension between the Communist guerilla army and the police erupted into violence and British troops were called in to support the latter. Michael was ordered down into Athens to open an Intelligence Office close to General Scobie's Headquarters in the Grande Bretagne Hotel. Thinking he'd only be gone for a day, he left most of his possessions behind, including his bulky copy of Stanislavsky's *My Life in Art*. His convoy was vigorously attacked on the way into Athens but ran the gauntlet successfully. They were luckier than the rest of the unit which was captured in Kifisia and marched away up north as hostages.

During Christmas dinner at the Grande Bretagne, which consisted of two slices of bully beef instead of the usual one, and was lit by hurricane lamps and candles, as the Athens power station was in Communist territory, a Greek policeman was taking a stroll in the sewer immediately underneath them and found enough dynamite to blow all the revellers sky high. Perhaps the Communists had expected Churchill, who had gone to Athens to see things for himself, to be at the hotel.

All this time, and while I was with ENSA, our letters never reached each other, and we both felt very cut off. Michael was sent from Greece to Odessa in a ship carrying Russian ex-prisoners of war liberated by the Allies in Western Europe and destined for the Gulag at best, there to pick up a party of Allied ex-POWs liberated by the Russians, and destined by contrast for a hero's welcome in the UK. The great thing for us, though, was that the voyage was to end in Liverpool – something which he knew, but of course I did not.

It was 30th March and he arrived at about midnight. In case the shock would be too great for me, he pretended on the telephone to be an American friend of his who had news of his imminent arrival. On hearing the American accent, I sleepily slammed down the telephone. (Many homesick Americans, after first showing photographs of their wives and children, hoped for a little sex life. Who shall blame them?) Anyway Michael rang again in his own voice. We were too excited to make much sense. He arrived the next morning. I opened the door and fainted. He was home for good.

14

Marriage is a difficult, even if rewarding, business. It is after all meant to be a commitment for life and we hadn't been together for any length of time for the last six years, and for the last two, not at all. Michael had left as a boy of twenty-four and a promising young actor, and returned a man of thirty – a Captain in Intelligence. I had been an inexperienced repertory actress when he left, and was now an established star. *They Were Sisters* was about to be shown in Leicester Square. If anyone bothered to talk to him at all when I was with him, they addressed him as Captain Gray. A non-star standing next to a star is treated like a pane of glass, almost exactly in the same way as is an old woman standing beside a young one.

He was so proud of me that he didn't seem to mind and I admired him for it.

Saint Augustine's definition of friendship seems to me a very good basis for a happy marriage. 'To talk and laugh with mutual concessions, to read pleasant books; to jest, to be solemn, to dissent from each other without offence, to teach somewhat, or somewhat to learn – to expect those absent with impatience, and embrace their return with joy.'

We are often asked the secret of our long marriage. How do we know? Perhaps it is that we have always been passionate friends, and we have a similarity of taste (awful to live in a home which made you wince every time you entered), and although we are very different in temperament we do have the same ideas about money. I am by nature undomesticated and Michael has never been in the least male chauvinist, so he helps with the chores, although I am now quite a good cook! Sex has never been a problem, and Michael is a good actor, which is important to me. We have a need to cherish and Michael is tolerant and amusing. I can trust him in essentials, and he is loyal in spite of many female predators. I think almost more important than anything, he has always left me the space to be myself.

I'm a born bolter. At my first school in Wallingford, I had run away but had been found within a few hours. At my third school, I broke bounds daily and daily met the understanding headmistress, who pretended not to notice that I was off limits and daily walked me home. In Malaya, I had run away for good.

Oddly enough, although it was hard to deal with at the time, I believe that the separation actually helped us. We had both married very young and, by being away from each other, we had room to grow. I carried on by myself with a life I loved. Poor Michael didn't enjoy the Army but he had been given a great deal of responsibility and had eventually found an Intelligence job for which he was well qualified.

Of course in a long marriage there are disagreements and rows and one both inflicts and receives grievous hurts. There are times of intense claustrophobia and a desire for freedom, and many many sexual temptations, but nothing is simple in this world. For most worthwhile things, one must work. And we are partners.

When Michael returned, we found that the flat was really too small for the two of us. We weren't rich (I had earned £600 my first year at Gainsborough), but the gods were with us and we were lucky enough to be offered a half share in a large Edwardian flat off Baker Street by the playwright Esther McCracken. She was moving back to her native Northumberland, and we were to share with Gladys Boot, an excellent actress, with whom we then lived for sixteen years.

Gladys became a great friend. She was a spinster, daughter of Canon Boot of Newcastle, and had been an amateur actress in Newcastle until Esther McCracken wanted her for her play *Quiet Weekend*. With great courage Gladys, whose father had just died, sold up and came south to earn her living on the stage. She remained stage struck but became totally professional and was highly praised by James Agate for her performance as Madame Ranevsky in *The Cherry Orchard*.

Her part of the flat was full of Victorian and Edwardian furniture from the canonry. Ours, to start with, had two deckchairs, two camp beds of different heights, an army blanket as a carpet and two beautiful Derby vases that I had bought in Cardiff; Gladys with great sensitivity brought in a deckchair when she visited. I hadn't dared tell Michael about the furniture in Inverness, but by immense good fortune, it was delivered soon after we moved in.

Curtains and carpets were impossible to get, so we bought dhobi weave, a strange sort of coarse linen for the windows, and a kind of thick orange tight-woven canvas, for the carpeting of the corridors. It wasn't pretty, but it was better than nothing, and our first real home.

The first of our three wonderful daily housekeepers, Amelia Wooster (Millie), came to us soon afterwards, too, and was to stay for thirteen years. Millie was very plain, as her drunken father had broken her nose by throwing her downstairs when she was a little girl but she forgave him freely, as she forgave us all, for all our sins. She was an East Ender who knew a free way to see almost everything worth seeing in London. Her boyfriend, an ardent Communist, was a lift man at Harrods.

Suddenly I received news that my brother Roger had survived his three and a half years of captivity in Singapore, and was on his way home. Michael met him at the station and we brought him back to the flat. He had had twenty-three attacks of malaria, he was very unwell, and had soon to go to St George's Hospital, and there he fell in love with a young nursing sister, Bess Holtam, and luckily for him she fell in love with him. They are still happily married.

Meanwhile, although the war in Europe was over, Michael had not yet been demobbed and was now told he was to be made a major and posted to Germany. Instead he managed to persuade the Army to let him transfer to Stars in Battledress where he ran an unusual drama school. Ballet classes in army boots were only one of the difficulties as they nearly brought down the ceiling of the room below. But among the Upper Grosvenor Street teachers were many who went on to become household names, such as Terry-Thomas, Cheerful Charlie Chester, Faith Brook and James Donald.

They Were Sisters opened in London and I had rave notices, especially from James Agate, then the most important critic in England. 'Hurray,' I thought, 'I'm made.' The telephone bell rang. It was the Gainsborough Studios.

Would I please come over as the Ostrers wanted to talk to me. Excitedly I went down the Polish Corridor and was sacked for being too realistic. I had insisted on looking frumpish and unattractive when driven to suicide, and in those days the convention was that you stayed looking glamorous and pin-neat, whatever was happening to you. I came back on the bus in tears. (As you can see I was not well paid! Also to rub salt into the wound the bus like most buses then had a large picture of me, proclaiming 'Rising dramatic actress'.) I sat down at home to have a real good cry in the hall. The telephone bell rang again, and it was Eric Portman to ask me to star opposite him in the film *Wanted for Murder*!

My relief in discovering there was life after Gainsborough Pictures received a further boost from Associated British Pictures who were planning to make a film of Francis Brett Young's celebrated novel *My Brother Jonathan*. They asked me to play Rachel, but there was no firm shooting date as they wanted an unknown young man to play the long leading part of Jonathan Dakers and couldn't find him.

'We've been running through scores of old film tests lately,' said Robert Lennard, the casting director, worriedly. 'We're at our wits' end, but there is a young man whom we can't find as we don't know his name, who has real potential, who did a test here with you in *Banana Ridge* back in 1942. I don't suppose you remember his name?'

Wild with excitement, but trying to look cool, I said, 'Yes I do. He's at home and he's my husband.'

Michael was about to return to the profession he had yearned for through six long years.

1946 began for me with the lead in an American play *Dear Ruth*, imported for the St James Theatre by the famous impresario Gilbert Miller, and for the first time I was put top of the bill. The play didn't succeed but, as I was at this time a critic's darling, my notices were excellent and I was engaged by Peter Daubeny (later to become the instigator of the exciting World Theatre seasons) to do sixteen matinée performances of a pretentious play called *The Wind is Ninety* at the Apollo Theatre.

Douglass Montgomery, a popular Canadian film actor, who had made a great impression here in *The Way to the Stars*, was to direct and play the lead. I was to play his wife. It had an excellent cast and rehearsed for six weeks at Bedford Ladies College. My daughter was to be played by the talented and adorable little girl who had already played my daughter in *They Were Sisters*. When we reached the Apollo for the dress rehearsal, we were astonished to find the set was 'imaginary'. The curtain rose on a gauze, showing a house with a verandah and a garden with a large tree surrounded by a circular seat. But when the gauze was 'flown' cast and audience were left to grapple with a navy blue limbo. There was a navy blue fisherman's netting as the backcloth. The verandah was a nine-foot navy blue rostrum reached by navy blue steps from the navy blue garden. The circular seat round the invisible tree was – also – navy blue. So were our costumes and even the felt soles of our shoes. Douglass played a dead American Air Force pilot and his sergeant – also a ghost – was played by Bonar Colleano. Both wore uniform and were spared felt soles, so that unlike the living, their footsteps on the boards rang out noisily.

Worse was to come. There was general anxiety before the dress rehearsal about negotiating the invisible stairs; Douglass who, though good-looking, appeared to have no sense of humour, looked at us sternly. 'Some of us are worried,' he said firmly. 'There is no need. Although I don't use the staircase, I will myself show you how easy it is to descend those stairs.' He climbed up, turned round and stepped with his left leg into space, and broke it. The shock was so great that for a few moments we were helpless with laughter. Douglass left for the hospital but we dress rehearsed early the next morning and Douglass, now swathed in plaster from knee to hip (not navy blue!), behaved with great bravery.

My life however was complicated by the fact that John Clements and Kay Hammond were acting *Private Lives* in the Apollo in the evenings and there weren't enough dressing-rooms for all of us, so I was asked to use Muriel Pavlov's dressing-room one floor up at the Globe next door. I had four quick changes, from a sixteen-year-old with a bow in my hair to a forty-year-old wife, and back twice. My passage to and from the theatre was joyfully greeted by the street traders and itinerant musicians who yelled encouragements, gave me wolf whistles and doubled up with laughter. It was difficult to feel immersed in the play. I also had to dance a waltz with Douglass, which I was now forced to do alone, but which Douglass insisted that I do dancing backwards as though I was still his partner. All in all, besides feeling nervous I also felt harassed.

The première had an even more daunting surprise for me. As the girl of sixteen I had to sit on the backless bench dreaming of Douglass, my girlhood sweetheart. I was in a spotlight and it was meant to be a touching moment. Then clanking up the stairs with his plastered leg came Douglass. He had decided to come up behind me, turn my face upwards, lean over from the back and kiss me. By sticking his gammy leg out straight, he managed the kiss but was totally unable to stand up again. The kiss became longer and longer. He became heavier and heavier to support, and I heard the beginnings of a titter. I tried to duck from under him but unbelievably found that my lips were stuck to his. I wrenched myself away, losing some of the skin, and Douglass managed to save himself from falling. Afterwards, he apologised for what had happened, saying that old-time matinée idols sometimes used spirit gum on their mouths to create a sexy shine, and he had decided to try it, too late for it to dry properly.

[94]

In spite of all handicaps, including the fact that I had never dared to ask what the title of the play *The Wind is Ninety* meant, I was offered a film contract by Alexander Korda as a result.

15

Korda was filming *Man About the House* in Italy. I hadn't been out of England for ten years and the trip sounded very exciting. I was to star with Margaret Johnston and Kieron Moore, and Leslie Arliss was to direct. I was sorry to be parting from Michael so soon, but now he was working and, before leaving England I managed to get to Sheffield for the opening night of Jack Priestley's *Ever Since Paradise* in which he was playing with a very friendly cast which included Roger Livesey and his wife, Ursula Jeans, with whom we became great friends.

From grey Sheffield where the trunks of the trees were black with grime, I went to London where we boarded a plane especially chartered for us to fly to Rome. We ran out of petrol (!) in Toulouse, where we had to spend the night, and only arrived in Rome the following afternoon.

The transition was magical. There were blue skies and blazing sunshine, the city was by far the most beautiful I had ever seen or ever imagined, and all the women of this conquered country were exquisitely dressed. Maggie and I from conquering England where clothes were still rationed looked laughably dowdy and we hastily had silk dresses made to save face. The food was ambrosia to our war-rationed palates. Huge steaks – in fact meat of all kinds – fish, fresh fruit and vegetables were available for the asking. Defeated Italy, at least in the society in which we mixed, still had a brilliant life style and La Dolce Vita was in full swing. We were invited to endless parties. Drink flowed. Drugs were always on offer and people made love in every position on every free space. There were flashing jewels, people spaced out, people incapably drunk and people being sick. At one party I was introduced to a female film star whom I had always admired who was now middle-aged and fat. I shook hands with her gingerly; she was stark naked with a boy on each knee. After the austerities in England, it was all a great surprise. The houses we visited were filled with magnificent furniture and with grave, deferential servants.

he New Look and a gondola, in
enice to film *The Glass Mountain*.
ur co-star was Tito Gobbi (below
ght), a lovely man who became
firm friend.

Above: Christmas festivities at the Colombe D'Or, St Paul de Vence, with painter, Manfredo Borsi, centre.

Below: *The Franchise Affair*, which saw Kenneth More's film début in a tiny part.

Some of our girl extras for the film were also on drugs; kept that way by their agents to ensure their exclusive services. Many were ravishingly beautiful. It was hot – for me a benediction. In the Grand Hotel, taxi drivers who waited for their fares in the hotel foyer drank on equal terms with the other patrons. Everywhere Maggie and I went the men shouted '*Bella, bella*' and pinched our behinds. (I preferred just the *Bella, bella*.)

We went by bus to Ravello in the mountains near Amalfi. The villa Cimbrone we were told was where Garbo and Stokowski had their love-nest. The villa Rufello, a few hundred yards from our hotel, housed a pretty American woman who had come to Italy with her husband and her psychiatrist. The psychiatrist had told her she needed sex but, unfortunately for him, so enthused her with the idea that she ceased going to him for analysis and fell in love with the peasant gardener instead – like the heroine of our film!

In my part as a prim Midland girl visiting Italy for the first time, I had to draw back my curtains on my first morning and gasp at the scenery. In the interests of my art, as we had reached Ravello at night, I decided to pull back the curtains exactly like the character I was playing and see how I would react. In my amazement and pleasure at the real surrounding scenery, I gave a gasp which would have been far too exaggerated on the screen!

Amalfi and Positano then were two beautiful little towns on the sea to which tourists never came. Ravello, in the hills, was utterly unspoilt. Leslie Arliss, the director, had brought his enchanting wife and daughter to Italy with him, and we all had a wonderful time. The most astonishing week of all was when our film company hired Pompeii for six days. With no-one there but ourselves, and with plenty of free time, I read Trollope each day in one of the little frescoed rooms. The sun blazed down outside. The sense of the past tragedy of the place was still enormously powerful, but the film crew worked and sweated and we all picnicked for lunch as though we were on any location anywhere.

When the work down south was finished, we returned via a lavish week in Rome, to England. *Man About the House* was previewed in Eastbourne. C. Aubrey Smith, Constance Collier, Burgess Meredith, Paulette Goddard and a host of English film stars were invited to the showing. We were all put into limousines with the inside lights on and cheered to the nines as we were escorted to the cinema by outriders on motor bikes. Eastbourne was astonished but the showing was initially a flop until Leslie Arliss re-edited. By the time it finally went out on general release, it was a great success.

My next film, *Mine Own Executioner*, overlapped *Man About the House*. I acted opposite Burgess Meredith who was at that time still married to Paulette Goddard, but they were not getting on well and things can't have been improved when a doctor Burgess consulted told him that he was allergic to Paulette's hair.

Now at last Associated British, Michael's new film company, took the plunge and cast him for the enormous part of Jonathan Dakers, in *My Brother Jonathan*. My own part was small but, as this film also overlapped *Mine Own Executioner*, it was probably just as well. There was in fact one fantastic day in May when all three studios wanted me. I had an early morning final retake at Shepperton for *Man About the House*, went to Worton Hall for an exterior shot on *Mine Own Executioner*, and spent the rest of the day at Elstree on *Jonathan*.

Although on *Jonathan* Michael was paid less than the head make-up man, things were looking up for us financially. We had our first car, a small red Wolseley, and we bought a three-year-old corgi, Bonnie, from a stud farm at Muswell Hill, where we heard he was going to be put down as he didn't enjoy his life in a small kennel serving bitches as his only recreation. Finally from the £1,000 left me in Mummy's will, we bought a little thatched cottage in Essex. It had a hundred rose bushes and a stream running through its half-acre garden, three enormous elm trees for shade and two orchards. There was no gas or electricity and no telephone. Behind it stretched large prairie-like cornfields. To one side was a farm and a village green, and it faced more thatched cottages. Michael, who had thought previously that Richmond was practically the jungle, was enchanted by the countryside and eventually took to gardening with great enthusiasm. We went there every weekend, and the flat arable land under wide skies was the perfect antidote to film studios.

At this point, Michael's dear uncle Jack Ballardie died. For him it really was a merciful release. He had found his nine years of paralysis almost insupportable. He was in constant pain. His devoted nurses thought that more than one whisky (his only solace) was not good for him. He never stopped grieving over his wife's death, and 'My God' as his only vocabulary was a great frustration for him. All through the war when I was in London, I had visited him weekly. He died before *Jonathan* made such a success, and was buried beside his darling Nellie in Petersham churchyard.

In 1948 we made *The Glass Mountain* together but, before we left for the Italian location there was a bizarre episode at the trade show of *Jonathan*. The trade show is for the exhibitors, their representatives, important cinema managers and the critics for the trade papers. In 1948 each reel of a film took eleven minutes to run and two projectors were used. At the end of each reel, a switch was made to the other projector. On this occasion, at the end of the second reel, Mary Clare, who played Michael's eccentric mother, became markedly more eccentric. Her clothes changed magically to flowing black robes and she began to talk excitably and incomprehensibly to totally new characters in unfamiliar surroundings. Mary Clare had been in two films shot simultaneously at Elstree, and a reel from the wrong film had been included in *Jonathan*. This didn't damp the enthusiasm of the audience and we left England for Italy knowing that the trade at any rate was solidly behind *Jonathan*.

We flew off in high spirits. In Paris we had a glamorous meal at the Ritz, then went on to Venice by the Simplon-Orient Express. There was then no air service to Venice. We stayed in Venice for two days before going on to Pocol, a village high above Cortina d'Ampezzo, where at the Hotel Argentina we met our co-stars Tito Gobbi and Valentina Cortese. Tito was leaning over the piano when we arrived, making suggestions to Nino Rota, the composer of the music. Between them Nino wrote a lovely and immensely popular score and became instantly famous.

Tito was irresistible. Good-looking, good-tempered, a splendid actor with a magnificent voice, he gave the film a class way above its station. He was a lovely man and became a firm friend. We are delighted to have been involved, however indirectly, in introducing him to the British public. Valentina, beautiful, dramatic and very urban, with an entourage consisting of her grandmother, Victor de Sabata (a great conductor but, though nearly as old as the grand-mother, rumoured to be Valentina's lover), a young man called Walter who was in love with her and was always threatening to go to Africa to forget her, and an Austrian Baroness, who acted as her secretary. Valentina would change her clothes several times during dinner which seemed odd for a girl who was playing a simple peasant, but she played it excellently and received very good notices, as did Tito.

In the Dolomites, Michael, who was a first-class skier, skied to his heart's content, while I sunbathed and read when I wasn't acting. The film kept on running out of money. In Venice the money ran out so completely that the filming of the opera in the story had to be continued all night until cash arrived from Bologna to pay the extras. In these circumstances Michael, who had to conduct the orchestra in the story, really had to do it which, in that exquisite pink and gold Teatro La Fenice, gave him enormous satisfaction. He was guided by Franco Ferrara, a gifted young conductor whose career we were told had been blighted by epilepsy so that although he could make studio recordings, he couldn't trust himself to conduct live.

One evening Tito asked us to go gambling with him, and we had to explain that we were being paid our salaries at home and had only £5 *between* us as pocket money. Currency restrictions were still in force. 'Never mind, come and watch me!' he said. Michael and I lost the thirty shillings we allowed ourselves almost at once and Tito too had an unlucky streak, so after a while we decided to go home. In spite of our losses, we were all in tremendous spirits. It was late. There was a full moon over the Grand Canal and we went home in a gondola. Tito, a Venetian by birth, began singing in that marvellous baritone voice of his, the simple and melancholy songs of the gondoliers. As he sang, the shutters opened in nearly every window of the houses on either side of the canal. Heads appeared and soon all Venice seemed to be listening. We too, gliding along quietly, bathed in moonlight, were wrapped in enchantment.

We returned to England to find pictures of Michael on the hoardings everywhere. By the moving staircases in the tube stations the graffiti boys had given him monocles, moustaches, beards, earrings and balloons coming out of his mouth expressing filth. *Jonathan* was doing big business at the Empire, Leicester Square, and my film, *Mine Own Executioner*, which had had considerable critical success, was in the cinema next door.

And now we made, to my mind, two irreparable mistakes. Michael was offered a part in *Lady Windermere's Fan* (to be called *The Fan* in the Hollywood film) by Otto Preminger, and Hugh Hunt offered us *Romeo and Juliet* with some other wonderful parts at the Bristol Old Vic. Either would have been a leap forward in our careers; the first giving Michael international stature, the second giving us much needed theatrical experience. Unfortunately, at the same time, Henry Sherek offered us two parts in *Rain on the Just* – a good new play by Peter Watling destined for the West End. Michael's part was excellent. Mine was dim. All three offers were pressed unremittingly and we ended up doing *Rain on the Just*. In spite of the fact that *Rain on the*

Just was greeted as a brilliant first play and Michael's performance hailed equally enthusiastically, I have never ceased to regret our refusal of Hugh Hunt's offer. One of my abiding regrets is that I have done too few of the classics and have been stretched far too little as an actress. It was a very real joy that Michael was now accepted as a good actor on film and in the theatre, but I had played three dreary parts in a row: the put-upon wife in *Mine Own Executioner*, the put-upon wife in *The Glass Mountain*, and the put-upon daughter-in-law in *Rain on the Just* and, although I hadn't had childhood yearnings to become an actress, now that I was one I didn't want to throw away my chances. On the other hand, we were together again and acting together, and Michael was at last in his longed-for West End.

Domestically however, we had an enormous slice of luck. Marjorie Fielding, who had been with us in Edinburgh and Glasgow and who had become a great friend, suggested that she, Gladys Boot and Michael and I should all share a house and so be able to choose something fairly spectacular. She suggested one of the Nash houses in Regent's Park. Michael and I were sent to scout and found that 39 Chester Terrace was on the market (so was a house in Cumberland Terrace, but its basements included cellars so large that they reached the limits of the park itself. This seemed 'somewhat too sensational' for us).

39 Chester Terrace was a four-storeyed whitewashed terrace house of great beauty. There was also a basement, a mews flat and two garages. There would be plenty of room for the four of us. Like all the others in the terrace, 39 had a lovely fanlight over the front door, fourteen-foot-high ceilings, long windows and large beautifully proportioned rooms. Its snag was that it was beside the archway to the rest of the terrace and had two houses opposite, so it didn't have an uninterrupted view of the park. It was however very cheap indeed, £4,000 for a seventeen-year lease. We had as yet no capital but Marjorie was to pay £2,000 for herself and Gladys and lend us £2,000. At the last minute, Marjorie decided that she didn't want to leave Dolphin Square. Regretfully we told the current occupier that on our own we hadn't the money. But she had already bought another house and so let us have it for £2,500. It took a day to move Gladys's furniture into the top of the house, where she had a self-contained flat for which she paid £3 a week; our stuff was installed in the rest of the house in half an hour. Friends lent us pieces and pictures, but

we couldn't afford to furnish the dining-room downstairs for many years.

We took our first holiday together at Christmas time, driving south through France until we reached St Paul de Vence, where Michael had remembered lunching with his uncle years before. The Colombe d'Or in those days had white pigeons in the garden, views over the hills of unspoilt countryside with a few olive trees and vineyards, a well with its bucket filled with a huge bouquet of flowers, celestial food and pictures on the walls by Picasso, Matisse, Modigliani, Bernard Buffet, Chagall, Marie Laurencin and Bonnard. Monsieur Roux, the proprietor, was a painter and his wife, Titine, heavily built, beautiful and sympathetic, was the perfect hostess. It had already become famous as a restaurant and its clientèle included Churchill, Gary Cooper, Yves Montand, Simone Signoret and Simone Simon, film directors such as Jacques Prévert, as well as many famous artists. At night it became the village pub; and the local tart and the local carpenter, as well as most of the village, came to drink.

One day several of us were having a drink with Jacques Cousteau on the terrace. Our table faced the open garden gates and the road up from the coast. Suddenly a magnificent white Rolls-Royce drove up. The back door was opened by a chauffeur and from it emerged a smirking and effeminate young man and then, with an enormous effort and very slowly, a hugely fat, very old lady with badly dyed red hair, a dead-white overpowdered face, bright blue eye shadow and heavily mascara'ed eyes. Her cheeks were brightly rouged and her mouth made up into a small red bow. Pink pearls the size of marbles were round her fat neck, and she was dressed in a little-girl style white dress. Her bolster-like legs were covered in wrinkled white stockings and she wore little-girl patent leather shoes. She was followed by a second contemptuously sniggering young man. They more or less dragged her to a seat and ordered drinks.

Everyone on the terrace, who had been shocked into silence at her appearance, now began to laugh. I'm afraid Michael and I did, too. Cousteau was displeased. 'How do we know why she is like this?' he demanded. 'Her story may be a tragedy perhaps. We do not know, and we have no right to laugh until we do.' How splendidly right he was.

We made great friends with Manfredo Borsi, a painter living in the village. He told us this, I trust, apocryphal story about Chagall some years later. It happened at the Fondation Maeght at St Paul. There was a big Chagall painting immediately to the left of the gallery entrance. Chagall enjoyed sitting in front of it and listening to the admiring comments. One day of pouring rain, no-one came into the gallery except little Master Maeght, the son of the proprietor, and some schoolfriends. On seeing Chagall they all said, '*Bonjour Maître*' in such a deferential way that the great man was charmed.

'Come here,' he said. 'I, Chagall, will make for you a picture. Fetch me paper, fetch me pencils, and I Chagall will make a picture just for you.'

The little boys bounded away delighted, and returned with paper and pencils.

'Now,' said Chagall, 'I will make for you any picture you like. What would you like me to do?'

The little boys bounced happily up and down, then Master Maeght said, '*Faites-nous un Miro, s'il vous plaît.*'

When the Colombe had been burgled some time before, only Borsi and Chagall had not had their pictures stolen. Both were humiliated, and for some reason they disliked each other from then on. Chagall claimed afterwards that his picture wasn't stolen because it was above a grand piano which would have been too much trouble to move and Borsi that his picture, made of lava and vitreous enamel, was too heavy to lift and impossible to roll up.

16

Farce acting is a very precise form of acting. Any blurred sentence fails to get its laugh. You have to believe in yourself and your predicament, as in any other kind of acting, and then deliver the lines utterly clearly and with exact timing. *Queen Elizabeth Slept Here*, our next venture, was a farce and a good exercise early in our careers. Though Ivor Brown, the critic, rightly said we were not natural farceurs, the show was a great success at the Strand and when we left it after nearly a year, it was still playing to packed houses.

A very strange thing happened on tour in Liverpool. At one moment in Act Two, when Michael was sitting in a corner with his back to the rest of the stage, a woman in brown walked on, sat herself on the sofa, pulled her dress over her knees, then walked off again. It was meant to be a lull in the otherwise phrenetic action, and no-one saw her; not Michael, nor Kenneth Connor (then in his twenties and playing an eighty-year-old gardener), nor I, who was the next one to enter. Nor indeed the stage manager. But in front, watching the show, was Talbot Rothwell who had anglicised the play which was originally called *George Washington Slept Here*. He was outraged and came thundering round after the matinée to ask why we had introduced a non-speaking new actress with a minute part, which meant nothing, into 'his' play. As we none of us had the slightest idea what he was talking about, an enquiry was made as to what could have happened. It transpired that the woman had escaped from a mental home, and had been pursued into the theatre by two warders and, after her brief appearance on stage, she had been run to earth in the gents' lavatory two storeys up.

After the London first night, we celebrated by taking Robert Lennard, the casting director of Associated British Films, and his wife, Kay, and Dickie Attenborough and his wife, Sheila, to Ciro's, where a short while before we had seen a girl in the cabaret chorus whom we had thought quite exceptionally good. Her name was Audrey Hepburn. As we had hoped, Bob put her under contract. Not that

British Films did anything with her except give her a tiny part in a film as a cigarette girl and then lose her to an American company who starred her opposite Gregory Peck in *Roman Holiday*, which made her a world star a year later.

The unhappy truth was that the post-war Government had sold the British film industry down the river by weakening the Quota Legislation which was the only protection available against the overwhelming international power of Hollywood. The Americans were our greatest rivals because they speak the same language – or, nearly. The Quota was designed to ensure the showing of a minimum proportion of British films in British cinemas – 45% in 1948, reduced to 30% a year later – but it was more honoured in the breach than the observance by many cinema owners. To make things worse the Quota defined as 'British' a film made in a British studio by a British company, with 75% of the cost going to British labour. However, in assessing this percentage, the salaries of one artist or one technician could be excluded, permitting a foreign star or director to be employed. The loopholes were legion; for instance a film could be shot by a British company entirely on location in Italy, with American stars, a French director, a Greek script writer and a few British supporting actors and technicians and yet qualify for the British quota. That wonderful film *African Queen*, with Humphrey Bogart and Katharine Hepburn, qualified as a 'British' film. No-one who sees it thinks of it as other than American. Laurence Olivier, Michael and I among others saw the dangers and tried in meetings and interviews to demonstrate them. We held a press conference in the hopes of making the press understand, and were accused of being anti-American. But Equity was right behind us. (Michael was elected to the Council of Equity in 1949 and served for twenty-seven years, becoming Vice-President three times.)

All we asked for was that, in order to qualify as 'British', a film should have within its 75 per cent labour costs at least one British star. The advantages would have been enormous. American-financed pictures made in our studios wouldn't have been damaged by the loss of British nationality, since they already had the entrée into 70,000 of the world's 90,000 cinemas and, if they weren't 'British', Equity couldn't object to American star casting. On the plus side a British star teamed with an American in a 'British' picture would be seen all over the world. If we had succeeded in our aims, it might have been at Denham and Elstree that Vivien Leigh, James Mason, Richard

Burton, David Niven, Elizabeth Taylor, Rex Harrison and Audrey Hepburn had their best opportunities.

We had dinner with an important American film producer who said that Hollywood wouldn't be unsympathetic to our proposals, but unions in the British industry were frightened that American film makers would be driven from our shores and their members would lose jobs. As a result, by the middle 'fifties serious British film production was in decline, and studios large and small were closing. A few independents, notably the Boulting Brothers, carried on successfully and luckily BBC television expanded and ITV came into being, thereby cushioning the job losses for actors and technicians. Rank and ABC who made 90 per cent of their profits from showing pictures, not making them, were more in favour of stepping up the flow of no-risk American pictures than of propping up the home article which, if it were authentically British, had little chance of a wide showing in America and too small a home market to pay its way.

In 1949 there was still a picture-going public who put British actors first, and Michael was placed fifth by popular choice in the *Picturegoer* Gold Awards. Laurence Olivier, Michael Wilding, Robert Donat and Alec Guinness were ahead of him and he was followed by Ralph Richardson, Gregory Peck and Alan Ladd. In 1949 the crowds had to be kept back from our stage doors by police.

In 1950 we made *The Franchise Affair*, a film based on Josephine Tey's excellent novel, in which Kenneth More played the tiny part of a garage attendant, and we went for a holiday in the South of France where we fetched up in the same hotel as George Kaufman who had written *George Washington Slept Here*. He was on honeymoon with Leueen McGrath, a very pretty English actress, and we met side by side on our balconies exactly like the set from *Private Lives*.

We had already agreed to play in a two-hander called *The Fourposter*, written by a young Dutchman, Jan de Hartog, who had married Priestley's step-daughter, Angela. It had six scenes with a time spread of over fifty years. This meant lightning-quick costume and make-up changes and, although we had accepted, we were very frightened of the whole enterprise. Jan had written the play in English when hiding from the Gestapo in an old women's hostel in Amsterdam, and when he escaped from Holland he had to leave it behind. He collected it again two years after the war. In the first scene where we had to be in bed, we were told that as we were married we could actually play it as written, but that we should be the first people for many years to be allowed to play such a scene without one foot each being on the floor.

It was a charming play except for a whimsy last scene which we never got right, but the tour was a great success. Just before we opened in Cambridge, Stanley French, our manager, told us that if we didn't invest in it, the play couldn't open. The publicity had already gone out, so we invested our entire savings which totalled exactly £400, and eventually made it to the Ambassadors. The critics were mixed in their reviews to say the least, but an American actress called Jessie Royce Landis came backstage in a state of great excitement to say that she knew it would be a great success on Broadway with us in the parts. Alas the negotiations floundered because the American impresario would only finalise contracts if we would agree to stay in the play eighteen months if it were a success. Associated British refused to let Michael go for more than six months, so the rights were acquired by that brilliant couple Jessica Tandy and her husband Hume Cronyn. José Ferrer directed and managed to get Jan to write a good and amusing last scene, and it became a huge success. It was filmed also very successfully by Rex Harrison and his then wife Lilli Palmer, and eventually made into a musical starring Rock Hudson. In spite of all this, we never got any money back from our investment, as our profits were used by Stanley French to buy a quite terrible new play which was offered to us and which we refused. He was a sweet man but a compulsive gambler in the theatre.

Fortunately we didn't realise at this time that our long streak of good luck was on the blink.

We were invited to the Film Festival in Uruguay – the first ever in South America – with Phylllis Calvert and her husband Peter Murray Hill, Glynis Johns, Bob Beatty, John Sutro who had produced *The Glass Mountain*, and two critics, Freda Bruce Lockhart and Matthew Norgate. Michael and I went off ahead of the rest as we wanted to see the pictures in the Prado. It was snowing in Madrid and scorchingly hot in Montevideo. Uruguay then had the hardest currency in the world. The rich were very rich and we were treated like gods. Uruguay is like Wales bathed in sunshine. We stayed in a large pink 'Elizabethan' hotel and we were each given a valet and a secretary. Sir Douglas Howard, the British Ambassador, was splendidly hospitable, and the organisers had laid on non-stop entertainment. There were six American, six French and six Italian film stars besides us, including Joan Fontaine, Gérard Philipe and Claude Nollier, and luckily for us *The Glass Mountain* was well received. Sir Douglas became a good friend and, years later when he came to live near us in Regent's Park, he confessed he had spent the last week before the war having dinner with Marshal Pétain on the Sunday, lunching with Kim Philby the next day and spending the following weekend with Guy Burgess!

Angels One Five had another dreary part for me but started the career of John Gregson, and extraordinarily enough it was Jack Hawkins's first starring part in films. During it, I had the first very faint intimation of some sort of malaise; I felt permanently but not dramatically below par but I took no notice and went to the Venice Film Festival with Anne Crawford as Britain's official representative. Beautiful funny Anne! She told me that she'd had leukaemia since she was twenty-one and 'was always having bits cut off'. She said it without a trace of self-pity and she was always the best and most amusing company in any gathering.

We were given the usual £5 as spending money and put in a down-market hotel, from which we had to take a tram to the Lido where all the action was. Flying the flag was not easy in those days. But Irene Dunne and Orson Welles were especially kind to us and lent us their cabino on the beach; and our trump card was that Anne lived in a basement flat in Hyde Park Gate opposite Winston Churchill's London home and knew him quite well. Of course everyone wanted to meet the 'saviour of Europe'. He used to come to the Lido to bathe (wearing a faded blue costume with a scooped neck, and 'leggings' which came to the knee), accompanied by two bodyguards. One of them patrolled the beach, hardly unobtrusive among the sunworshippers in his blue serge suit, and the other bathed with him. As he arrived, all eyes feasted on him, a small tubby man with a pink face and white legs. 'Ah! The beautiful white legs of Mr Tourtshill!' sighed the women. Churchill entered the water and, when out of his depth, turned on his back and floated, with his stomach sticking roundly out of the sea. His bodyguard swam round him like a porpoise.

At lunch in the fashionable little restaurant across from the beach, he had a special table reserved for him and he used to sit at the end of it facing the door. Everyone greeted him and he just nodded, but for Anne, and therefore for me, he was most welcoming, so our stock was high. Fortunately we were wined and dined by someone for every meal!

One day at lunch, Churchill was sitting by himself at his table in the restaurant, and one of the little ragged boys who used to run in and out stealing bread rolls or whatever they could, in a kind of game of tag with the waiters, actually sat himself down beside Churchill. The head waiter was aghast and prepared to eject him, but Churchill boomed, 'Let the child stay.' They then both carefully chose what they wanted to eat. Churchill tucked his napkin into his collar. The child did the same and they both tackled the food with great enthusiasm. Both obviously enjoyed themselves enormously, but they uttered no word to each other, foreign languages never having been a priority with either of them.

A highlight of the Festival was the Bestigui ball. Bestigui was an antique dealer who had bought a magnificent palazzo, the inside walls of which were covered in Tiepolo murals. It was a fancy-dress masked ball and everyone arrived in the moonlight by gondola in their lovely shining dresses. Jacques Fath, then perhaps the top Paris designer, had made most of the women's clothes, and it was one of those occasions when everyone who was anyone was there. But the British delegates weren't allowed to go to the ball, as the affair was supposed to be unegalitarian and liable to arouse bad feeling. No-one had explained this view to the Venetians who watched with delight in the square facing the other side of the palazzo where, in the best profligate tradition, a fountain was flowing with wine. There was a balcony on this side of the palazzo where the revellers showed themselves from time to time. Orson Welles, wearing only a tall white toque with his white dinner jacket, was immensely popular, and Jacques Fath and his wife, dressed as the Sun God and Goddess in white and gold, received tremendous cheers – until they took off their masks, when the crowds groaned to find they were no-one they knew. No bad feelings about anything else were aroused by this particular display of wealth, and I much regret that we were forbidden to accept our invitation.

The delegations from all the other countries gave great dinners or balls or lunches for everyone at the Festival. The British only gave a cocktail party before lunch on a Sunday and yet Anne, looking enchanting, had been proud to accept a prize for *Trio*, one of the films entered by Britain only a few nights before, and was a great favourite. It was all very embarrassing.

17

Since the first day I trod the stage, I'd had good fortune and an exceedingly busy life. My notices were invariably good to excellent and, as I had become aware when doing my audition for the Webber Douglas, I felt securely at home as an actress; indeed an actor's life fits the bill extraordinarily well for a variety of people, always providing they are dedicated, not afraid of hard work (when they can get it), and have what Sarah Bernhardt called 'un certain petit talent'. For the shy, as I have already pointed out, it is almost a therapy; for the show-off, a godsend; for the intellectual, full of riches to be mined; and for the intuitive, it provides a way of responding to a variety of interesting stimuli.

For me, with my need for a mask behind which to hide, combined with an urgent wish to please, it is tailor-made. My abiding difficulty though was, and is, my appearance. I have always hated my face and as, when a young actress, I was nearly always cast as a pretty girl or woman, I went through many moons of despair – and a good deal of make-up!

I don't know why I am so acutely discomforted by my looks – perhaps because in my institutionalised period at St Anthony's, when I was naughty, as I often was, I was always warned, 'If you can't be pretty, be good'!

The 'fifties, however, were for me the most alarming and depressing decade of my life so far. For Michael, fortunately, they were very different. However, in 1951, before the difficulties proclaimed themselves, I had one of my most unlikely but most rewarding critical successes.

Sandy Wilson, now famous for *The Boy Friend* but then unknown, came to see me in Chester Terrace to ask me to star in a late-night revue at the Watergate, a tiny fringe theatre which held a maximum of ninety people. The revue was to be called *See You Later* and Sandy was to write most of the material. I told him that I had a very unattractive singing voice, absolutely on the note but sounding like an angry wasp, also that I was sick of being a good little nonentity in small parts which in no way deserved the large billing I was given. So we dreamed up an opening number in which, dressed in the demure costume of a Dresden shepherdess, with a pretty straw hat with bows and ribbons, hooped skirts, white stockings and buckled shoes, I gleefully praised a garden full of Indian hemp and other narcotics. He also wrote a song called 'Michael Denison Slept Here', sending up the his 'n' hers image we seemed to present, and finally included a wonderful take-off of Mistinguette, called 'Mademoiselle Suzy Sans Doute'.

We had quite a time in rehearsals as the director was suddenly called by God to become a monk, and the clothes designer's mother died, so we had to make our own clothes. Once under way, it wasn't a particularly happy engagement either, as the other two girls in our minute dressing-room made it plain that they despised my film star status. On the bright side, Charles Ross was one of the men in the show and he and I began a lifelong friendship, and soon the lovely June Whitfield replaced one of the girls. We were (or I was) paid £6 a week for ten sketches in the show starting at midnight and, after a terrifying first night which began with the curtains refusing to part, and Michael gallantly 'paging' the right-hand one to and fro – and the other one falling to the floor – the revue had an excellent press and my own notices were fantastic.

Kenneth Tynan came breathlessly round to my dressing-room after the show to tell me that I was nothing less than superb. (He was not at this time a critic unfortunately.) He said he was directing a Grand Guignol Season at another tiny theatre, the Irving, and asked would I play all the good girls in it. He said he would send me the script at once.

I was feeling really ill by now and, as the Irving season meant I would be playing virtuous heroines again, and also that I would be doing sixteen different parts in two different theatres starting at 7.30 and finishing in the early hours of the morning for £12 a week, I most regretfully refused. He was furious and sent me a very rude letter saying that he would be getting an 'actress, not a film star' to replace me. In the event the 'actress' and Ken had extremely bad notices, and Ken never forgave me.

Michael meanwhile was filming *The Importance of Being Earnest* with Michael Redgrave, Edith Evans, Joan Greenwood, Dorothy Tutin and Margaret Rutherford, directed by Anthony Asquith. A wonderful film, almost perfectly performed.

Perhaps here I can interject one of my favourite stories about that great actress Edith Evans.

She had a 'set' (as the flats in Albany are called) which she wished to redecorate and asked a friend of ours if he could recommend a good interior decorator. He suggested a young man he considered brilliant, but who had had very little experience. Edith told the young man that she had no ideas at all about how she wished her place to look, but that she was going away on holiday for a few weeks and wanted it finished by the time she returned.

When she came back, he had indeed finished his work. He had furnished the drawing-room round a beautiful Sickert which he had hung over the mantelpiece. The curtains, carpets and soft furnishings either matched the colours in the picture or complemented it. The young man showed her into every room and she professed herself delighted. Then they returned to the drawing-room.

'You are really pleased?' he asked anxiously.

'Delighted,' she replied.

'Even here in the drawing-room?'

'Certainly.'

The young man looked embarrassed. 'May I ask you something?' he enquired diffidently.

'Of course.'

'I found that Sickert in your bedroom.'

'Yes?'

'Yes.' He stumbled a little, then went on, 'It was behind the wardrobe.'

'Yes?'

'May I ask why?'

In that magnificent swooping musical waterfall of a voice of hers, she replied confidently, 'Well, I don't know. I suppose it was because there was a hook there.'

Later I learned from Binkie Beaumont that the picture in question was a Sickert portrait of Dame Edith herself, which he had for years been trying to buy for the foyer of the Globe Theatre.

In January Michael and I had a short holiday in Majorca, in the then only large hotel near Palma. The little country airport smelled of broad bean flowers, and I began writing a play which at that time I called *Take Copernicus*.

: Arriving in Montevideo in our English winter clothes en route to the film festival in Uruguay with the left) Phyllis Calvert and Glynis Johns.

: With (from the right) Norman Wooland, Rosamund John and Jack Priestley who directed his own *Dragon's Mouth*.

Above: With Michael and our corgi, Bonnie, at the top of the ladder and Jack Hawkins below in a publicity picture for *Angels One Five*.

Above: Home was a Nash terrace overloo Regent's Park. We were happy there for n years.

Below: *Love Affair* which began so promisingly turned into a nightmare. From the left, Julie Somers, Mic James Grout and Dulcie.

We came back to rehearse *Dragon's Mouth* by Jack Priestley and Jacquetta Hawkes (soon to be his wife). Completing the cast were Norman Wooland and Rosamund John. Jack called it a 'Platform Drama in Two Parts'. It had been inspired by a reading in New York of *Don Juan in Hell* (part of *Man and Superman*) by Charles Laughton, Agnes Moorhead, Charles Boyer and Cedric Hardwicke, and had what Tynan called 'some of the best rhetorical prose' he had ever heard. Jack was an old friend. Jacquetta rapidly became one, and we all set to work with excitement and optimism.

We had been rehearsing for a few days and Michael and I were lunching with Jack at Albany where he had two sets, one of them B4 (where Ernest from *The Importance* lived!) – when Thane Parker, the company manager, arrived very flustered to see Jack, and we offered to leave. Jack told us to stay, and Thane then revealed that Jack's wife, Jane Wyndham Lewis, had left him for a 'bird watcher from the North' and wished to divorce him. After a few moments of total disbelief, Jack became very funny about the bird watcher and asked us to spend the following weekend with him. He would invite Jacquetta and her son Nicholas, he said. So on the Friday, all five of us drove down to 'Brook' (the full name was Brookhill, but Jack called it Brook), Jack's enormous house in the Isle of Wight. Jack was nervous for some reason but defiant. 'I'm a generous man,' he kept saying. 'I've told Jane to take anything she wants, but she's not that kind and she'll not want much.' He was wrong.

We arrived just before dusk and Jack took a huge old-fashioned key out of his pocket and turned the lock. It was a cold evening, and we all followed him inside the house thankfully. Downstairs was almost empty. In the room immediately on the right, only a pianola was left. There was very little furniture in the drawing-room, the dining-room was practically bare, and the walls had few pictures. Jack was astounded. So, I may say, were we. Upstairs there were beds and chairs, and the bedroom Michael and I were to sleep in looked cosy and charming. We none of us said much. There was too much to say, so we changed quickly and went down to dinner. But from that moment on, Jack became a wonderful and wildly funny host. He plied us with food and drink and sang and danced, and told us hilarious theatrical stories, and kept up this non-stop and totally endearing entertainment all weekend.

One of my favourite stories about Jack dates from before we knew him but is a true glimpse of the man himself. In his days with Jane

Wyndham Lewis, it was their custom on the Monday of a weekend full of guests to give them a tour of Jane's farm, and the pièce de résistance was her prize bull. On this particular weekend they had had a poet to stay with his little boy who was dressed, poor child, in velvet with a lace collar, looking like Little Lord Fauntleroy. Jack took exception to the wretched child immediately. When at last they reached the bull, Jane went into a long and enthusiastic description of his prowess in serving cows. The poet became more and more worried, finally he burst out, 'Please, please Jane! No more. My little son doesn't know the facts of life!' Dancing with irritation, Jack shouted 'Then don't tell him! Don't tell him! They're too good for him!'

Jack directed *Dragon's Mouth* himself – he was a good director and when the time came to tour, he hired an old-fashioned red bus to take us all over England for one-night stands in various town halls. I think his dream was to recreate *The Good Companions*. I used to be very car-sick so, to Jack's disappointment, Michael and I decided to go in our own car. In the event it was a fortunate decision because the bus driver had absolutely no sense of direction and, day after day, he lost his way and poor Rosamund John and Norman Wooland, the stage management, and the understudies arrived at their destination frustrated, exhausted, and with no time to rest before the show.

It was a splendid play to do. It said some pertinent things about the differences in the sexes and gave a Jungian insight into four very different ways of living.

After six exhilarating but tiring weeks, we opened with our four-character play at the unsuitably huge Winter Garden in London – now demolished. In spite of this, we had a very good press. John Barber said I was superb but by this time Ken Tynan was the *Observer* critic and he found words of praise for the writing but gave me the first of a series of hostile notices of my work over the next decade.

In the play, all of us were facing possible death from a tropical virus, but we never knew who would die. One very fine day in June, I went to see an eminent Harley Street specialist about the constant pain and swelling I had in my stomach. My throat glands were also slightly swollen and painful too. I had been to a doctor in Cambridge, who had given me the consultant's name, and I was feeling more and more ill. The specialist was an impressive-looking man, heavily built with a profusion of greying hair, a rounded stomach and a shining face empurpled by good living. He wore a morning coat, a bow tie and striped trousers and treated me, and I'm sure all women, with gallantry and an exaggerated patience. He was after all dealing with the second sex. I told him how I felt and he said, after kneading my stomach, taking my blood pressure and doing various tests, that he would like to talk to my husband. I replied that it was I who was suffering and I who had come for his opinion. I still have a kind of amnesia about the rest of the consultation, but some minutes later I found myself walking back to Regent's Park, in brilliant sunshine, under a bright blue sky in a daze of incredulity and rage. He had told me that I had advanced stomach cancer and eight months to live. (I know now that he himself was becoming mentally ill. He soon afterwards told a woman patient suffering intense pain, vomiting and such severe pre-menstrual tension that it rendered her unfit to work, that he too had great discomfort every month.) But at the time I believed him and was outraged to know that I was to die so young. When I reached home, Michael was out and by the time he returned I had resolved not to upset him by telling him what had happened. I thought I could handle the situation myself – at least for some time. It was one of the stupidest things I have ever done.

I suppose most adolescents growing up imagine a death scene for themselves. I certainly did. Pale and angelic looking, I should be lying against the pillows with a heavenly choir in the background and grieving relatives and friends round the bed. Facing the reality was very different. Why I hadn't insisted on a second opinion, I don't know. Michael would have done. Mesmerised, I suppose, by the bow tie and striped trousers! My chief emotion was this great rage. I took a deep dislike to the world outside my home. I suffered from insomnia, and I was so shrewishly bad-tempered that I can't imagine why Michael, in ignorance of the situation, stayed with me. Luckily we were working solidly for the entire eight months.

After the run of *Dragon's Mouth*, we did a charming and light-hearted film called *There Was a Young Lady* (produced by Michael's old colonel, Dick Rawlinson) which gave Geraldine McEwan her first part in films and had a bevy of excellent character parts played by stalwarts like Kenneth Connor, Sydney Tafler, Charles Farrell and Bill Shine. It was directed by Laurie Huntingdon who had directed *The Franchise Affair*, and it was chosen to accompany the film of the Coronation on general release.

Then we did a play with Marie Löhr who was still a big star and had once been a theatre manager. She was a lovely woman and a brilliant comedienne. We were deeply shocked at being billed above her and I told her so. In her deep bass voice which had an attractive crack in it, she said, 'Ah, my dear, I can see you are very emotional. I am so emotional that I even cry when I send my carpets to be cleaned!'

The play was called *Sweet Peril* and had been written by a very pretty blonde American who wanted to play Michael's ex-girlfriend in the play. She was not allowed to do so, which in the circumstances was to prove fortunate. We set off for our prior to London tour in good shape as far as the play was concerned, and I was feeling no worse in health. We opened late in 1952 at the St James's Theatre, then in the hands of Laurence Olivier and Vivien Leigh.

The part Michael played was a weak womaniser and drunk, who had been in love with a pretty American blonde before the war. She had broken off her engagement to him when war was declared and he still pined for her. On the rebound he had married a staunch and loving little woman (me) and he spent most of his time gazing at his old family home through binoculars from his tumble-down cottage, instead of working hard on the smallholding he owned. Michael, who by now usually played solid citizens, went to town on this characterisation.

The blonde American playwright then wrote to her own ex-boyfriend to say that she had written a play about him and her and his wife, and that it was on in London at the St James's with Michael and me in the cast. The boyfriend asked a lawyer to come to the show and we were off on the Saturday. The oddest thing of all was that Michael had been at Harrow with the boyfriend and had no idea that he was acting him.

On the night we came off, we went to bed exhausted. Margot Stevenson (who had played the ex-girlfriend) was staying with us. At about two a.m. we were woken by the telephone and Michael answered it. A man with a rough accent said he was speaking from Savile Row police station and would we come down to identify and bail out Nigel Patrick and his wife Beatrice Campbell. Groaning, Michael dressed and went out. Although I was half asleep, I suddenly realised that the caller had pressed 'button A', so the message had obviously come from a public call box – not a police station. The telephone rang again. Alert now, and frightened for Michael, I picked up the receiver. The same voice said, 'We've watched Michael leave the house, and we're coming to get you.' There was then a string of obscenities. I put down the phone and went to tell Margot, who was fast asleep after a very heavy end-of-play party and couldn't be woken, then I went upstairs to warn Gladys what might happen. She was sitting stiffly upright in bed, having heard all the filth on the telephone (we were on a party line), and she told me to bolt the front door. 'They might be able to open the lock,' she said. 'They can on television.'

I rang the local police and 999 and quite soon both lots arrived; the local police having already arrested the Chester Terrace night watchman, a surly man who had enjoyed fighting in the Boer War and who, as an old soldier, had instinctively taken cover in some laurel bushes.

When Michael arrived back after a very embarrassing visit to Savile Row police station, Gladys, all the policemen and I were having tea in the kitchen.

The following day with Margot more or less out for the count still and Michael out playing golf, I suddenly realised that the eight months were up and I wasn't dead. On the Monday I went for a second opinion at last and was given a clear bill of health. Among other things, I was suffering from overwork and exhaustion. The relief was so great that I collapsed with a nervous breakdown and went to University College Hospital.

18

I spent two or three weeks in hospital and was put first on sedation, then given pills at night. I also had a session with Dr Tredgold, the hospital psychiatrist, with whom I struck up a firm friendship, and in the following years I gratefully consulted him on the behaviour patterns of psychopaths when writing my crime novels.

He told me some very interesting things. He said that he believed most psychiatrists came to their jobs because they had some intense personal problem themselves to work out. In cases of an unhappy love affair he would say to his patients, 'Abandon Hope All Ye Who Enter Here' – like the words carved over both the entrance of Dante's Inferno and the doors of the Victorian mental hospital, Bedlam. When I looked shocked, he said that in a love affair one of the lovers usually loved more profoundly than the other and would find it nearly impossible to change the heart and mind of the other if things became intolerable. So the unhappy one was the only one who could change the situation. Abandoning hope therefore was the only answer. Obviously excellent advice, but pretty hard to follow!

Which brings me to my writing.

I had always wanted to be a writer. As a child, I had written various little books and illustrated them – at Wallingford, chiefly about horses or mice, both of which I found easy to draw, but about which I knew nothing, though I anthropomorphised the mice. I wrote a version of *Beauty and the Beast* too, and acted both parts at its only performance! At the holiday home in Norfolk, I had tried my hand at a detective novel and in Malaya I had had my gossip column. The years since my return to England had left little time or indeed the inclination to write, although there was the play I had started in Majorca.

I now followed my spell in hospital with a long holiday at the Colombe d'Or in the South of France where I had set *Take Copernicus*. I took the opportunity to finish the play and then resumed writing in earnest. I did quite a lot of television in the 'fifties, and found that I enjoyed it very much. In the autumn of 1953 I went into a strange

[118]

play by James Parrish called *The Distant Hill*. Maurice Teynac, a very attractive young French actor, came over from Paris to play the part of my husband, an eccentric puppeteer, and we wandered round the provinces playing to not very large audiences for several weeks. I found I had plenty of time on tour for writing – especially at night, because then and for the next ten years, I was an almost total insomniac.

I wrote the first draft of a play called *Love Affair*, based loosely on my art school days at Ozenfant's, and started on what I hoped would be a radio play for our darling lodger Gladys Boot. As Gladys was still very pretty, and an extraordinarily good sweet woman, well known for these qualities, as well as for her gentleness, I thought it would be fun to write a murder play in which she could be a murderess. She too was ill at this time and frightened that she wouldn't get any more work. Unfortunately the play turned itself into a novel and, half way through, as the old woman was going up the stairs to commit her murder, she herself was murdered (I had no idea by whom!), so I put the script away for the time being.

Michael and I then acted together in a play called *We Must Kill Toni*. It read well but played badly. It is very difficult indeed to judge a play solely by reading it. Even a rehearsed reading is not the same as playing to a paid audience. Perhaps it is a question of the impact of the situations in the play, which become more immediate and more important when acted. (Even Jack Priestley, experienced as he was, always believed his latest play was his best after he had written it.) Though it is the writing that matters most, casting, direction, acting and sometimes the sets, can affect a play for better or worse. Anyone connected with the stage will tell you, 'If we could judge plays accurately, we would all be millionaires.'

Because I had agreed to do *Toni*, however, I was unable to accept an offer to play Mrs Elvsted in *Hedda Gabler* with Peggy Ashcroft – which I much regret as she is an actress I admire inordinately, and Ibsen a playwright I adore. Our play also had a very bumpy ride as the management kept running short of money and paying us in cash out of suitcases. A joint television engagement followed in *Olympia*, by Molnar, directed by Stephen Harrison, with whom I worked often and happily, then we did a Royal Variety Performance at the Palladium.

Straight actors are at a grave disadvantage in Royal Variety Shows. They are used to 'being someone else', and to the creative interpretation of a character. Unless they can sing and dance, therefore, they are usually seen at their worst, but the occasions are fun. It is lovely meeting such a broad section of one's colleagues, to feel the years of grease paint behind the stand-up comics, the juggling acts, and the show-biz glitz, fun to meet the great American stars too. But a little show-biz goes a long way with me – like publicity, I enjoy it very much in short bursts. Then I like retiring behind my mask.

After this we went to Dublin in *The Fourposter* and while there were invited to take the play to South Africa, which seemed a good idea as I was still depressed by my continuing insomnia.

In response to our request to be allowed to play to both black and white audiences, we were told that at the City Halls up and down the country – and we would be playing several – there was no ban on mixed audiences, although the blacks never attended through lack of interest and lack of money; but that it was whites only in the theatres. We flew to Johannesburg and were driven down to Cape Town through the Great and Little Karroos.

South Africa is probably the most beautiful country I have ever seen. That veteran opponent of apartheid, Alan Paton, gave a mocking title to his last book, *Ah, But Your Country's Beautiful*. It is. I had been expecting an arid brown landscape, under sunny bright blue skies. Instead much of it is green and lush. Huge lilies and red hot pokers stalk down the hillsides. Shocking pink and yellow pig-flowers bloom everywhere. Graceful trees bear canopies of scarlet blossom. In Zulu-land, which is tropical, there are waterfalls on the Insusi River behind which you can sit on little ledges, in the shade of a smooth green curtain of water, and the Zulu women sing mournfully among the clusters of their whitewashed and thatched rondavels. Their men are all away in the mines. At night the skies glow with outsize stars, so crisply brilliant against the soft indigo canopy curving over a darkened world that they seem almost within reach.

We opened at the Hofmeyr Theatre in Cape Town, then went on tour through the Eastern Province with bathing things and a picnic in the back of the car. In the country districts it was almost impossible to realise the nature of the regime under which the black and coloured people lived. It seemed pointlessly cruel to subject such a courteous and willing people to so much indignity. In Johannesburg it was worse. We didn't perform there, but the iron bars on the windows, the pass laws, the enforced separation of black couples acting as servants was horrible. In spite of overflowing hospitality, we hated the place and, although we loved our management and ever-generous hosts, Brian and Tweets Brooke, we were glad to say goodbye.

It was now 1955 and Michael's dream to play at Stratford in Shakespeare came true, largely through Laurence Olivier's kindness. They had been together on Equity for six years and liked each other. In 1954 it was announced that Larry and Vivien would be heading the 1955 season, and Michael wrote to Larry to ask him to put in a good word for us both. He did and, as a result, Michael was offered Fenton in *The Merry Wives*, Bertram in *All's Well*, and Lucius in *Titus Andronicus*. Michael agreed, although the parts were ludicrously unsuitable for him. He was nearly forty and all of them were juveniles. Sadly, all the possible parts for me were already cast. Bertram in *All's Well* is Shakespeare's most unattractive hero, Fenton a vapid drip, and Lucius has little to offer except that he survives the holocaust at the end. In the event Michael played Sir Andrew Aguecheek in *Twelfth Night*, with Larry as Malvolio and Vivien as Viola, Lucius in *Titus Andronicus*, Dr Caius in *The Merry Wives*, and Bertram in *All's Well*. He was a very good Sir Andrew (which had led Glen Byam Shaw to switch him to Caius), but *Twelfth Night* had only mixed notices.

Ken Tynan was gunning for poor Vivien and she knew it. He described her performance as 'Dazzlingly monotonous' and she with her precarious mental health was thrown into a deep depression. John Gielgud who directed the play read the notices with horror and said, 'Great heavens! After this no-one will ever work with me again' – a pause, then – 'except Edith at a pinch.'

Larry and Vivien were wonderfully kind to us and, as heads of the company, they behaved impeccably; but Vivien's health, both mental and physical, was causing them both acute worry, and Ken's implacable hounding of her was indefensible. He can't have thought her a really bad actress, her performance in *Gone With the Wind* alone entitled her to his respect, and indeed Larry wrote in *Confessions of an Actor*, 'I told him that he had been directly responsible for at least one of Vivien's nervous breakdowns.'

Larry also wrote, 'The severe critic gains respect by being feared, and his approval is much coveted; in order to win such prestige the quality of his writing has to be immaculate.' Later he goes on, 'His destructive weapons were deadly, strengthened by the scintillating quality of his writing. His praise was equally impressive, but rarer of course, because bitchiness is the journalist's handiest tool.'

In order to be taken so seriously, Ken had to attack the top people.

He was known as a 'fearless' critic. What had he to fear? He had a solid, very well-paid job. It was the performers he attacked who needed to be fearless. Their livelihood and future were at stake.

Larry and Vivien headed the 'beautiful people' of the day. They lived in a 'glorious abbey' as Larry called Notley, an atmospheric mediaeval house surrounded by acres of farm lands. They were the most famous pair in the world and were loved and revered in the theatre. In 1955 it all ended; not publicly until a few years later – but in fact.

We had one quite ghastly weekend at Notley. The horror started in Vivien's dressing-room, where I went to see her after watching *Macbeth*, and to tell her that Michael and I were ready whenever she and Larry wished to start. There was a peremptory knock on the door and Ken appeared. He stared at her in silence in apparent hatred and contempt – then left the room, not having said a word. Vivien who, up to that moment, had been chatting and laughing, crumbled into frightened tears. I left her with her dresser and went to Larry's room where Ken was almost grovelling with praise and flattery to Larry. The following two days were a nightmare. Vivien, shocked and scared, was working herself up into a state of rage and despair. She would allow no-one to go to bed until the early hours of the morning, and gave me such enormous and powerful whiskies with nowhere to throw them away that I had one of my very few hangovers the next day.

The next day she was ill with pleurisy, and at lunch to which I only just managed to struggle and where I was the only woman with Larry, Danny Kaye, Orson Welles, Tony Bushell and Michael, I could hardly eat.

After lunch Michael and I went for a walk in the blazing sunshine, and then slept under a hay stack. Vivien attended by doctors was in bed, and Larry was in the garden wih Danny Kaye. Suddenly Larry was with us and we talked for half an hour or so before turning for home. There was a strange noise of great festivity. 'My God!' said Larry. 'It can't be!' But it was. Vivien had got out of her sick bed and had rung up about fifty friends, all of whom were drinking noisily and happily with her. We burst in on the party. Vivien looking radiant and, apparently in her early twenties, waved at us happily. The party lasted at full strength until five the next morning. Larry, who was to play Malvolio that evening and was also in the process of cutting *Richard III*, was paste-white with exhaustion. So was Michael.

I left for London and a television job, looking 105 (Vivien now looked seventeen), and Michael went back with the Oliviers to Stratford.

One last memory of this Stratford year, which was wonderful for us as well as awful, was the first night of *Titus Andronicus*. There were always parties after the first nights to which Vivien loved going and Larry didn't and, as we lived close to the theatre in digs at the 'Old Ferry House' with a darling couple called Mr and Mrs Shakespeare (who once entertained a Mr and Mrs Macbeth to tea on their lawn), we gave him an open invitation to use our little room for a quiet drink while waiting for Vivien's party to finish. We ourselves sometimes went out and sometimes didn't. On this particular night when we came back from a party, he was there with Noël Coward, Johnnie and Mary Mills, Vivien's parents, Mr and Mrs Hartley, Emlyn Williams and a few others. Noël was in top form telling stories in his inimitable way, and the atmosphere was very festive. The first night had been a sensation. The audience had come expecting to jeer, but from the moment they heard Peter Brook's music, they became fascinated and, at the end, they all stood in homage to Peter and Larry. The next day Larry would be hailed as the greatest actor in the English-speaking world. Noël stopped speaking and Larry started a story. He was a good raconteur but as circumlocutory in the telling as Noël was brief. All the time he was talking he kept his eye on Noël, and when the punch line was delivered to delighted laughter, he looked relieved and pleased. 'Larry,' I said in amazement, possibly a little drunk after my party, 'you were watching Noël all the time you were telling that story. Does it really matter to you so much if Noël laughs or not?'

'Certainly,' replied Larry quite seriously. 'Noël was my first leading man, and the gap never lessens.'

How's that for humility?

Dear Larry! What a complicated man he was. Blazingly talented, quite often feeling himself an 'upstart' for some reason, he brilliantly led the theatre for more than forty years, although it should never be forgotten that it is John Gielgud who with Binkie Beaumont's help gave him and Edith and Peggy, Michael Redgrave, Alec Guinness and many others the crucial career-building opportunities of their early years.

Larry described Marilyn Monroe as schizoid. Perhaps all actors are – certainly to some degree Larry himself was (as was Vivien). Kind, ruthless, sophisticated, naïve, funny, charming, immensely hardworking, inordinately brave and inordinately ambitious, a powerful thread in his make-up was yet humbly high Anglican, and 'confessing' was a part of his nature.

19

The autumn of 1955 saw the production in Birmingham of my own play *Love Affair* at the Alexandra Theatre. We had planned no more than a reading of it by members of the Stratford company to an invited audience at Stratford, but when we learned that Derek Salberg wanted something for the Alex, we sent it to him and he accepted it. This was exciting beyond my wildest dreams. Maxine Audley and Keith Michell agreed to play the leads – they were perfect casting, and two absolute unknowns, Ian Holm and James Grout, were also in the cast. It was a time of high hope, although I hated doing the auditions as I was so acutely conscious myself of the hell of rejection.

The play, then in two acts, went very well in Birmingham and J. C. Trewin wrote a long and constructive notice in the *Birmingham Post*, and John Barber's criticism in the *Express* was headlined 'Good! Try again, playwright Dulcie.'

This brought Henry Sherek to the scene. Henry was the lovable gargantuan theatrical impresario – passionately interested in modern plays – who had put on *Rain on the Just*. He liked what he saw at Birmingham and bought my play with two stipulations, both of which we should have refused: one, that we should have a happy (and inappropriate) ending, and two, that Michael and I should play those parts so absolutely right for Keith and Maxine. We foolishly agreed (Keith and Maxine weren't available anyway), and Henry told us he would put *Love Affair* on in the spring.

We ended the year with *Alice Through the Looking Glass* at the Chelsea Palace. Michael repeated the parts he had played the previous year – the White Knight, Humpty Dumpty and Tweedledee. I took over from Margaret Rutherford as the White Queen. This may sound odd casting, but I have played many outsize character parts. What is acting about if you can't play different kinds of people? Good parts can be played in many ways. That is why Shakespeare is so attractive to actors. His wonderful parts admit such widely variable interpretations. And it wasn't as if I was taking over the White Queen during a run, so I could bring my own interpretation to the part. Juliet Mills, a natural-born actress at fourteen, played Alice. Those great stars of the past, Leslie Henson and Binnie Hale, played the White King and the Frog Footman and the Red Queen. It was a privilege working with them.

Through them I began to realise that age had one further humiliation for actors; they had to take small parts to keep going and to do it with grace and dignity. Marie Löhr, Lilian Braithwaite, Cedric Hardwick, and now these two, all playing poor parts because so few good parts are written for the elderly. All of them passed the test with flying colours.

So 1956 arrived and with it Henry's production of *Love Affair*, with its additional third act. All his improvements were based on a wealth of managerial experience. All contributed to a disaster. The ten-week tour gave little inkling of the troubles ahead. Audiences were large and appreciative and, of the twenty-four major provincial reviews, two were bad, three indifferent and nineteen good. The *Derby Telegraph* went so far overboard as to prophesy that our production could be 'the shot in the arm the theatre needed'.

First nights are total hell, but this first night was inevitably more frightening than usual, especially as Michael was also directing. We reached the Lyric, Hammersmith two hours before curtain up and Grace, who always dressed me then, was already in my dressing-room. Flowers were everywhere. I have a superstition about heather – actors are ridiculously superstitious – and Grace told me that not one sprig had reached the dressing-room; she had removed them all. I began my make-up with the usual dry throat and quaking knees. Various people from the management and the theatre came in to wish me luck. Michael and I gave each other our usual good luck signal. The five-minute call came over the tannoy, the noise of the audience arriving was switched on and it sounded like a good house. Suddenly the telephone in my room rang. I picked up the receiver and a voice I didn't know said, 'Is that Miss Dulcie Gray?'

'Yes.'

'You've never met me. My name is Heather and I'm ringing from South Africa to wish you luck.'

Shaking, I thanked her and, with a kind of despair, joined Michael and we went down to the stage together.

At first all seemed to be going very well. In the new third act though, there were one or two odd laughs when my heroine produced a revolver. At the curtain call there was solid applause, and then from the gallery we could hear boos. It was terrifying. We took as few calls as possible and staggered back to our rooms. Mavis Wheeler, who had just come out of prison for attempting to shoot her lover, Lord Vivian, came round with him to my dressing-room to say that the shooting scene was totally truthful, and a few other brave souls said they had enjoyed the play, and that was all. There were silent fans outside the stage door. I can't now remember if Michael and I went out somewhere. I suppose we did. It is all a blank.

The next morning first thing, Terence Rattigan rang.

'Don't let those boos fool you,' he said. 'They came too soon and too pat. They were organised. I've been in an audience many times when there have been boos. They never all start at once, nor so soon. They straggle and then gain confidence. It was a phoney demonstration. Don't take too much notice of the reviews, either.'

I thanked him, dazed and miserable.

The notices were mostly very bad, and most mentioned the booing – understandably. I turned trembling to Ken Tynan's review which then shattered me but which I now find cheap and silly. He wrote '*Love Affair* is a callow study of sex in a Pimlico art school, written by Dulcie Gray, directed by Michael Denison, and starring Michael Denison and Dulcie Gray. This division of labour shatters at a stroke three cardinal rules: that actresses should not write plays, that playwrights should not act in their own work and that directors should not appear in their own productions. It also suggests a fourth rule: that actors should not marry.'

He was a brilliant writer – sometimes an outstanding critic, but he was also malicious and subjective; the subject being the rise and rise of Kenneth Tynan. My play probably deserved most of what it got, but with Ken as leader of the pack the critics bayed like dingoes. One even said it was obvious I had never been to an art school!

The telephone rang again. Again it was dear Terry. He was so enraged by Tynan's review that he took me off to the Society of Authors for an opinion on whether it was actionable. They thought it almost certainly was, but advised against taking action. It was a humiliation at the time but of course it was only a few weeks' wonder. Had I gone to court, the stench might have lasted a long while.

I put the episode behind me and pulled out *Murder on the Stairs*, the play that had turned itself into a novel, and resolved, come what may, to be a writer.

Shortly afterwards, I was offered *Tea and Sympathy* in Australia and Brian Brooke, in England at the time, offered me Noël Coward's *South Sea Bubble* in South Africa en route, and I thankfully accepted.

Michael as always was rock steady in his comfort and understanding. I got a grip of my murderer and finished *Murder on the Stairs* and it was accepted by Herbert Van Thal for publishers Arthur Barker.

Our happiest engagement ever, *Candida* at the Oxford Playhouse in 1961.

Above: Left, the chorus line at the Palladium in a Night of a Hundred Stars with (standing left to right) Je[a] Kent, Thelma Ruby, Dulcie, Joan Sims, Miriam Karlin, and (in front) Janette Scott, Pip Hinton, Sheila Si[x] right, more decorously as the Duchess of Hampshire in *Let Them Eat Cake*.

Below: Drinking to the success of our Allied Theatre production of *An Ideal Husband* with (from the le[ft] Perlita Neilson, Roger Livesey, Margaret Lockwood and Richard Todd.

20

While I was away, Michael, thank heavens, was busy acting – this time for Henry Sherek at the Edinburgh and Berlin Festivals.

South Sea Bubble was to play in Cape Town for several weeks and Joss Ackland, then very young and inexperienced but already a good actor, was to play opposite me. Apartheid was more overt now and, while I was there, the beach in front of the hotel which had a lovely sandy shore was suddenly divided by a wooden breakwater. On one side whites could bathe. On the other side blacks. As no blacks ever bathed there, this was gratuitously insulting to them, as well as stupidly halving this beautiful bathing area for the whites. In the local papers, there was a call for more white immigration, side by side with a diatribe against the British. Before I left for Australia, I gave a thank you party at the Country Club, inviting two of my favourite people who were Jewish. I discovered that Jews were not accepted there. Truly a strange country! So beautiful and so full of hate.

From Cape Town, I flew to Sydney via Mauritius and Cocos, then the longest hop on the world's scheduled services. At magical little Cocos, there was a sign near where the plane landed which announced 'one foot above sea level'! The island reminded me of the East Coast of Malaya and I revelled in being there.

I was astonished on arrival in Sydney to find that I had been billed as a scarlet woman. Apparently *Tea and Sympathy* was considered a very daring play. It is true that as the schoolmistress in a boys' school, to help to persuade one of the boys to remain heterosexual, I opened the top button of my blouse but as a gesture this didn't seem to me to plumb the depths of wickedness. There were photographs of me with black hair, looking sultry and smoking through a long cigarette holder. There were photographs with my already well defined bosom, enlarged. *Tea and Sympathy* had been banned in England it is true, and had only been played in a Club Theatre – but it was by no means titillating – simply a well-made but not very highbrow play. The press conference was a huge one, and the wildest questions were hurled at me. One was – 'Do you always act in banned plays, Miss Gray?' 'No, of course not.' 'Why not?' Me wearily, and wryly, 'Because there aren't enough of them.'

Headlines screamed throughout Australia, 'Dulcie Gray wants more banned plays to act in,' and I was even preached against in the churches.

We opened at the Princess Theatre in Melbourne – quite successfully. The play was treated as an intellectual one. My cast were wonderful. Neil Fitzpatrick and I still write to one another around Christmas. I found an astoundingly pretty flat vacated by the American dancer Katherine Dunham, in a little Regency house near the Toorak Road, but it had some peculiarities. To begin with it was over an Indian restaurant where there were huge murals of naked Indian women with only a scarlet caste mark between their eyes as decoration. The whole place smelled of curry and at the turn of the stairs on the ground floor there was always a dirty mackintosh on the coat rack.

Upstairs everything was in old gold and scarlet, but the chairs, sofas and bed had been fitted with wood under the cushions and the mattress, as Katherine Dunham didn't like sitting or sleeping on anything soft. Violet, a remarkably nice English woman with a moustache, looked after me with great care. She was as homesick as I and loved talking to me about England.

Life for me in Australia was a strange mixture of happiness and hell. My insomnia was at its peak, and various doctors came and went in the effort to make me sleep. I was given sleeping pills of every conceivable colour; electric blue ones, dark blue and white ones, completely white ones, scarlet ones, pink ones, and yellow ones. I was injected, given morphine, and finally a hypnotist was tried.

The session with the hypnotist, who kindly came along after his performance in a variety bill in Melbourne, was funny in its way, but also depressing. He began by turning out all the lights except the ceiling one, which had its shade removed. I lay on one of the hard sofas, and was told to look at the light. I was informed that clever people make the best patients. I was then asked to clasp my hands lightly together, and told that I would not be able to unclasp them. I couldn't. We were both much encouraged. I was told that I felt sleepy – I didn't – that I wanted to raise first my right arm and then my left. I raised both. Encouraged again, I was told again that I felt sleepy – I didn't – that I wanted to raise my left leg. I didn't. I didn't go into a trance either and, although I often clasped my hands lightly and could not unclasp them, nothing else really worked, although my engagement ring began going out of shape with the strength of my efforts to unclasp my hands. Finally exhausted, the poor hypnotist left me (to sleep I hope) and I went to bed still wide awake.

My tiredness was appalling, and produced a more or less constant despair. I would walk round my flat crying feebly, and mouthing my lines from the play, in case exhaustion affected my memory. It never did. I felt like a zombie in a grey polluted world, but when I was given a morphia-induced rest, or the pills suddenly worked, I revived, and life became wonderful again.

I gave two inadvertently wild parties in Melbourne. I meant to give the parties but hadn't counted on their development potential! The first was for the combined casts of *Tea and Sympathy* and *The Reluctant Debutante* in which my friends Roger Livesey and his wife Ursula Jeans were playing the harassed parents. We invited about fifty people. By the end of an hour we had a hundred. Anyone who knew a party was on arrived with a bottle to join us. We had beer, Irish and Scotch whisky, gin, sherry, vodka, brandy, crème de menthe, cherry brandy, kummel, Williams (a pear liqueur from Switzerland), apricot brandy, Glen Moranjie and Tia Maria. You name it – we had it. No-one was sick, thank God, but people were passing out, petting, dancing, screaming, talking and singing, and music was going full blast. It lasted non-stop until about three the next afternoon. The same thing happened at my farewell party. It was exhausting, exhilarating and went on far too long, but was strangely well mannered and great fun.

The play rolled on for several months, then moved to Sydney and, on my last day in Melbourne, I was given seats for the Olympic Games. I was now writing my second novel, *Murder in Melbourne.*

In Sydney, which I loved, I had a good deal of trouble with a slightly deranged small part player in the company who kept on threatening me with murder, as he professed himself madly in love with me; and also a sad and curious time with Jessie Matthews who was out there playing in *Janus.* She was in a highly hysterical state and talked to me endlessly about Sonnie Hale, her first husband. As she and I were both English, she demanded my company all the time, but as I didn't know Sonnie and her marriage to him had been before my time, I found the whole business not only tiring but worrying, as I thought she needed the help of a professional psychiatrist. She had been Britain's greatest musical film star when she was young and of course

I wanted to help her, but couldn't. Then she quarrelled with her young landlord. She was living on his houseboat moored in one of the bays in Sydney harbour. After one quarrel more violent than the rest, he cut the painter, then jumped off the boat and she floated out to sea and had to be rescued by the coastguards among a good deal of publicity.

From then on she wanted to share my flat, but I refused as I knew it would be fatal. It was all very distressing and I was delighted when she returned to England, having recovered, and very happy that she so enjoyed her last years acting on radio in *The Archers*.

Travel not only broadens the mind but makes some of us a trifle unhinged, I think, which is why we travel with so many photographs of home, to remind us who we really are.

Alas, I could only spend nine weeks at home as I had promised Brian Brooke, who had been so kind at an important time for me, to return for a Johannesburg season of *South Sea Bubble*, again with Joss in the newly built Brooke Theatre. Michael was doing the first of his legal series, *Boyd Q.C.*, which became such a success that he continued for a further seven years. It was wonderful being home – and too soon to go away again, added to which I didn't like Johannesburg, but there was nothing for it.

South Sea Bubble was a play about the Governor's wife of a British-owned Pacific island (me) and the black Prime Minister and his clever son Hali Alani (Joss). The second act is a duologue at night, in a beach hut, between the Governor's wife and the Prime Minister's son. Both get a little drunk, and the young man a little amorous. It is a very funny act and in Cape Town got many laughs. On the first night in Johannesburg, it was received in total silence, but when the Governor's lady hits Hali Alani on the head when he tries to kiss her – usually the biggest laugh of all – the entire audience stood up and cheered.

1957 also saw the publication of *Murder on the Stairs*, with welcoming reviews in the *Sunday Times*, the *News Chronicle* and *Queen*, and much encouragement from Julian Symons, a writer I greatly admire. I finished *Murder in Melbourne* and started on *Baby Face* about a psychopathic killer, set in South Africa.

Our dear old friend Rosie Headfort was now mortally ill with cancer. She lived in Elsworthy Road, very near Regent's Park, and when the pain became too great, would invite me for a 'scrambled egg' supper. It never was scrambled egg – always caviare or pâté de foie gras or something delicious, served on a tray in her bedroom. Rosie looking very pretty still, in spite of her illness, was propped up in bed in a charming bed-jacket with an Edwardian headband of roses round her forehead. I used to try to talk her through her pain until some form of pain killer or sleeping pill could take over. She told me about her past, about how a specially chartered train would wait in Paddington to take the stage-door johnnies from the Guards regiment back to their barracks in Windsor – Lord Headfort among them – and how affairs (which she pronounced '*affaires*') were called 'tuck-ups' in her day; and of how, when she had a lover after she was married, Lord Headfort allowed her to spend three weeks a year with him on his yacht, provided that she remained a wife for the rest of the year, and was totally discreet. The lover used to brush her long hair in the sun on deck, a hundred times a day.

Rosie died, and has left a lasting gap.

To another young friend, I am told she spoke of the ludicrous difficulties of conducting an affair when she was a girl. The clothes they wore in those days were enormously complicated to remove. There were rows of buttons down the back, buttons at the wrist, and fastenings at the neck. There were petticoats which fastened with tapes at the back, corsets which took a long time to undo, and sometimes voluminous bloomers; stockings, garters and buttoned boots as well. An over eager or shy lover who set to work on the buttons at the back could also add to the time considerably. Yet after all this, etiquette demanded that the woman had to demonstrate her modesty by fainting with surprise – because it was all so sudden.

21

Michael and I started 1958 acting together in a television production of *The Importance of Being Earnest* with Tony Britton and Martita Hunt. One of the good things for us has been that we have been employed frequently in all the acting media, radio, television, stage and films. Basically the stage is the mother of them all and, in my view, although all the others play to millions more people, it is the most important one for an actor. All the media require truth, clear diction, creative imagination and an inner energy, but beyond that it is mostly a question of projection. The more projection required, the harder it is to portray truth, but if one can achieve this in the theatre, the scaling down for the other media is relatively easy.

All four media have their very distinct differences of course. In radio the voice is all, so it must be a particularly flexible instrument; also it must fill out for the listener all that he wants to know of a character, so that his own imagination can paint a satisfactory portrait. On the stage (the only visual medium where the actor still does his own make-up), one has to think clearly to the front of the dress circle. As one is in 'long shot', i.e. the whole body is seen all the time, posture, gestures, mannerisms and the essence of the actor himself, are all part of his characterisation. Nothing can be hidden as the camera can hide it – but equally a really 'close shot' of his face is impossible so, unlike in the two camera-dominated media, the face isn't all important. 'Remember,' James Mason told me, 'that in close-up on the cinema screen your face is roughly eight foot high by six wide – so don't do too much with it. Raise an eyebrow and it rises a foot. Act through your eyes and think through them.' Television is, in a way, the most life-like medium, but in both films and television, the camera itself chooses whom it likes. With some faces, however irregular, it falls in love. Others it rejects. It confers beauty and withdraws it. But just as a writer must love all his characters, good and evil, small or large, so must an actor. 'Star quality' is something else again. It is a kind of magnetism which keeps the public interested.

[134]

For me, one of the chores of filming was the amount of publicity one had a duty to endure. Television more or less generates its own, and the personal appearances connected with it are done for charity or money – both rewarding! Film personal appearances were unpaid and, if badly managed, could be acutely embarrassing. Dennis Price once sent us a very funny letter of apology. He had apparently lost his temper one night in Manchester. It seems that several cinema managers for whom he had been appearing in connection with a new film had actually introduced him to their audience as Michael Denison. He and Michael had started their film careers at much the same time, had become well known at the same time, and were more or less the same age. Both had a somewhat suave manner, both were good-looking, and both had Denis (though spelt differently) in their names.

At the last of the cinemas on a tiring and boring evening, the manager, after introducing Dennis as Michael, turned to him and said roguishly, 'And what do you suppose your dear little wife Dulcie Gray is doing at this moment?' 'She's probably in bed with Dennis Price,' replied Dennis briskly.

Talking about acting in general – apart from the frequent rejections we have to endure, by directors, management and critics – one of the hardest things to adjust to is being a new boy or girl so often. Few jobs last long, and too few have casts which contain old friends. As one grows older, this matters more. Interviews for jobs, too, I find very difficult. Talking one's way into work or blowing my own trumpet is for me an embarrassing business. I prefer to get a job from a previous piece of acting.

Still we don't have quite such a terrible time as some eighteenth-century actors. Charles Burney in Vienna collecting information for his history of music wrote, 'Fees are no longer given to actors who voluntarily submit to be kicked and cuffed by members of the audience. It was but a few years ago that comedians used to charge: So much for a slap on the face; so much for a broken head; and so much for a kick on the behind'!

Our television of *The Importance* could in no way compare with the lovely film Michael (who was acting Ernest not Algy this time) had already made, but it was fun to do – and the rest of the year was Charles Ross year. Charles, who had made a success in *Airs on a Shoestring* after *See You Later*, had become a composer, a London theatre manager, ran a car-wash, and two restaurants. He was a gifted and delightful man and died of cancer of the tongue. A horrible death.

For Charles I toured with Michael in a thriller called *Double Cross* and when Michael had to leave, Terence Morgan took over and we came to the Duchess Theatre and flopped. After this Charles, who had been adapting my first play *Take Copernicus* as a musical, put it on for a short tour. He wrote charming music and lyrics, renamed it *Love-à-la-Carte* and directed it himself. Like a coward, I adopted the nom-de-plume of Alan Chester as the author (the Chester part after Chester Terrace where we lived), and it toured briskly and successfully. In Richmond, Evelyn Laye bought an option on it. Alas, Charles and I were too inexperienced to make the changes she wanted, but it was a very happy time. Then again I toured for Charles in that excellent play by John Osborne and Charles Creighton, *Epitaph For George Dillon*.

I very much admire John Osborne as a writer but never saw the particular pleasures of *Look Back in Anger*. To me it seemed rather a whingeing sort of play, but his realism certainly started the new wave here, and very interesting that was and still is. The odd thing about the theatre is that each time an actor or a writer 'invents' a new realism, it is always hailed almost hysterically. Kean, Macready, Irving, Olivier – all were more 'real' than their predecessors. And yet this very realism has the seeds in it of becoming almost more old-fashioned than the run-of-the-mill acting. But it stimulates the imagination, and has far-reaching results and benefits. I've done few 'new' plays. Most of us would like to embrace every sort of play, so I regret it. John Gielgud, Ralph Richardson – and finally Larry himself – had their careers rejuvenated by acting in them.

While I was away Michael ran into Frank Hauser at Baker Street Station.

'The very person I wanted to meet,' he said to Michael. 'Can you and Dulcie come to Oxford to play *Candida*?'

So, with Jeremy Brett as Marchbanks, we did, and it was the beginning of our happiest engagement ever.

Frank was in the third of his sixteen distinguished years as director of the Oxford Playhouse, and what a joy he was to work for! We rehearsed for three weeks and played for three – and three very successful weeks, too. Michael and I both love Oxford. We saw a good deal of Tom Boase, the president of Magdalen, a good friend and a keen and perceptive theatregoer, and, when the play was over, Frank and Michael and I all promised each other to do *Candida* again somewhere, somehow – a promise that was kept two years later.

First Michael plunged back into *Boyd Q.C.* and I rested. Resting is a most untruthful way of describing being out of work, which is thoroughly restless and also painful, not only because no money is coming in, but because one is treated by everyone else as suffering from a contagious disease. Working actors fear they too may catch it. The public feel you're a failure. So do you!

I had introduced Michael to painting in oils on a holiday in France, and at about this time there was an exhibition of actors' paintings for charity, with a late-night private view. Earlier we had been to the Midsummer Banquet at the Mansion House, at the invitation of the Lord Mayor – an old schoolfriend of Michael's. It was a most glamorous evening with court dress, decorations, trumpeters and gold plate. We were accordingly dressed up to the nines. I even wore a lovely stage tiara. We went straight from the Mansion House to see the pictures, and there Emile Littler, who was casting a play called *Let Them Eat Cake* and looking for a couple to play the Duke and Duchess of Hampshire, saw us and offered us the parts! There was to be a short tour starting in Oxford, then we were to come in to the Cambridge Theatre. The cast Emile had found were experienced and wonderful – Phyllis Neilson Terry, Henry Kendall, Claude Hulbert and Guy Middleton (whom I had last acted with in *A Man About the House*) were some of them. Our white cross-bred labrador Titus, whom we had acquired during Michael's Stratford season to replace a much lamented Bonnie, was to play the dog 'Hants'.

We opened in London the day after John Osborne's *The World of Paul Slickey*, and we were all nervous that our frankly old-fashioned play would be given the thumbs down. It had been written in the late 'thirties by Frederick Lonsdale and had been scheduled for production with Laurence Olivier, but Lonsdale couldn't finish it to his satisfaction so, not unnaturally, it was dropped. It was a play of manners with a very visible French window, and so anathema to the New Wave, but in the event *Paul Slickey* was disliked and *Let Them Eat Cake* well reviewed, but a long hot summer defeated us.

Michael's real father died this year. He was a very good-looking neat little man; kind but weak. He lived with his second wife in Enfield. She had the money and it was her house. He had come back into Michael's life when Michael was in the Army, and he and I met from time to time at the Waldorf Hotel in London, usually for tea. He worked at Bush House. Both Michael and I liked him but Michael, although interested to come across him again, reserved his filial feelings for darling Mr Ballardie, and I couldn't help feeling shocked that Michael had heard no word from his father on his twenty-first birthday or at his wedding, and so couldn't feel unreservedly affectionate.

The 'fifties also saw the end of our attempts to have children. During the war, we had been almost thankful that we had had none, but from the moment of his return we wanted our own family. Unfortunately, it was not possible. We then discussed adoption but, although Michael had had a wonderfully happy adoptive childhood, we decided against it. Michael would have made a lovely father.

My last venture for the year was an extraordinary and ill-fated play called *The Best Cellar* about vampire bats. Almost everything was wrong with it except the really beautiful clothes and the début of Julia Foster.

Baby Face was published and well praised. Julian Symons, reviewing it, said, 'one of the most convincing portraits of a murderer in recent crime fiction', and Rebecca West came up at a party to say how much she had enjoyed it. It was the start of a lasting friendship.

22

The 1960s were as good for us both as the 'fifties had been bad for me. We were almost constantly in work and together, which we always enjoyed. People seem to find this hard to understand but, as we enjoy each other's company and enjoy work, it seems obvious that we should enjoy working together. Learning lines at home is easier, travelling is easier, meal times are easier. Nearly everything is easier, though first nights are doubly nerve-racking.

It was basically a theatre decade for us. We decided to make touring with plays an important part of our work if possible. During the war, theatres up and down the country had been very well attended. People needed entertainment to keep up their morale, not just in London. After the war, unscrupulous managements had traded on this goodwill, and too often provincial theatregoers were offered productions de-scribed cynically as 'prior to London' when they were nothing of the sort, or fraudulently as 'with full West End cast' which meant no more than that the company had been recruited in London.

By the 1960s the touring situation was becoming serious. Added to this there was a vogue for pulling down old theatres of eight hundred to a thousand seats, and replacing them with smaller ones, usually less attractive and with worse acoustics. Their smaller capacity meant that many of them were not viable for good London tours (especially not for musicals), as they couldn't pay the actors proper salaries on such truncated receipts.

We became patrons or 'friends' of various regional theatres – the Grand in Blackpool, the Royal, Newcastle, the Opera House in Manchester, the Royal Court in Liverpool, and so on, and spearheaded companies to keep the buildings standing. Twenty years later, most of them, thank God, are still there. We gave recitals in 1990 at the Grand Theatre, Blackpool, and also the Lyceum in Sheffield to help raise funds. Both theatres were being entirely refurbished. Very exciting. In the 'sixties the Lyceum could have been bought and refurbished for £150,000. Now it is to cost twelve million.

In the Victorian and Edwardian eras as well as during the 'twenties and 'thirties, touring was treated as a matter of course by the profession. The provinces after all feed London, both with talent and with their audiences, and actors then considered it part of their job to tour. We gave an interview to a Manchester journalist about our ideals, and the public excitement over the matter was both moving and surprising.

With Frank Hauser enthusiastically behind us, we decided to mount a tour of *Candida* and *The Importance*, playing two weeks at each date. We went to Joe Hodgkinson of the Arts Council Drama Department, who said that the proposal would have to be put to the Council but assured us that it would be a mere formality. (We needed only £2,000 as the production of *Candida* was already in existence for the two plays.) We then went to Peter Donald (our first employer) who was now Chairman of Howard and Wyndham which controlled a string of major theatres in Scotland and the north of England, and he agreed to book us for the spring and summer, so it appeared we were under way. After giving an interview to the *Stage* and announcing that the enterprise would begin with a week of *Candida* at the Bath Festival, we took a short holiday in Brittany.

We returned to find that the whole plan had fallen apart. The Arts Council apparently thought that we had simply dressed up a good job for ourselves and refused to fund it, and Howard and Wyndham, though prepared to book for their theatres, were not prepared to back a double bill of Shaw and Wilde – as being too highbrow. We were left with the one week at Bath. Frank had found a marvellous cast, as usual. Michael was still to play Morell of course and I, Candida.

Jeremy Spenser, a young actor of great magnetism, took over from Jeremy Brett as Marchbanks, Gillian Raine was to play Prossie, Ken Wynne was the new Burgess, and Greville Hallam was to play the part Michael had played on our wedding day – the curate, Lexy.

The play was almost sold out at Bath when we arrived and we opened to a very enthusiastic house. After the first-night party, Michael and I returned to our hotel and were just going up the stairs when to our amazement we heard a measured voice below us describing the evening in glowing terms and naming Jeremy, Michael and me most favourably. It was the critic of *The Times*, telephoning his notice.

His words had the most astonishing result. The current play at the Piccadilly was a flop, so the theatre manager there immediately asked us if we would open at the Piccadilly the following Monday. This was easier said than done, as Frank was not allowed to use Oxford Playhouse funds outside Oxford (one reason we had needed Arts Council backing), and a transfer to the West End also needed a member of the Society of West End Theatre Managers to present it (their initials unfortunately read SWETM!). What could we do? A couple of months previously I had acted in a television play of Somerset Maugham's short story *Winter Cruise*. In it was a handsome young actor called John Gale, who told me that he wanted to be a theatre manager and that if I ever had anything I wanted to do, he'd love to put it on – so we telephoned him and said we had both a play and a London theatre going begging, and asked him to present us. John saw a special rehearsal of *Candida* and at once agreed. So having publicly professed our eagerness to tour, we were back in London after one week!

The Piccadilly was much too big for *Candida* but the lovely play worked. We transferred in four weeks' time to Wyndham's, and there we broke the long-running record for the play and John Gale went on to great things. It was one of the happiest engagements we have ever had.

We did the promised tour after the London run, and from beginning to end spent a rewarding year. Michael followed this with a fourth season of *Boyd Q.C.* and I did another Maugham on television, *The Letter*, which was the play I had discussed with Maugham at Rosie Headfort's lunch all those years ago. Both the Maugham plays were produced by Peter Willes, who later at Yorkshire Television put on some of the best and most innovative plays then seen on television.

Michael and I worked together again in *The Bald Prima Donna* and *Chairs*, an Ionesco double bill for Frank Hauser at Oxford, and then started rehearsals for *Heartbreak House*, also with Frank, at the Lyric Theatre, Hammersmith. Roger Livesey played Shotover, Judy Campbell was Hesione, Michael Hector Hushabye. I played Lady Utterword and Perlita Neilson, Ellie Dunne.

We had been rehearsing for about a week when a very macabre incident occurred. The actor playing Boss Mangan was John Salew. Michael, who was sitting around waiting for his cue one afternoon, found a pile of yellowing newspapers backstage and began idly looking through them. One was a 1938 *Daily Express* and on the front page was a review of a play called *Death on the Table*, which included a favourable notice for John D. Salew. At the end of rehearsals, Michael showed the paper to John who confirmed that it was indeed an old notice of his. We all expressed astonishment at the coincidence and parted for the day. John died that night in the train on his way home. Sad and horrible.

I had a dresser aged ninety when we reached Wyndham's. Her favourite 'lady' and 'gentleman' were Gladys Cooper and Henry Irving, whom she claimed to have dressed at the Lyceum. She had made up all sorts of rules for herself which couldn't be broken, and one was that if I had visitors she must leave the room and sit on the stone stairs outside. I hated her doing this because I thought she might catch a chill. However I couldn't stop her.

One evening, a very good-looking clergyman from the Actors' Church Union came during the performance to tell me of his proposed visit to the Holy Land about which he was greatly excited. Although I love visitors at the end of a show, I dislike them before and especially during. Acting is being someone else and it snaps the thread to have someone unconnected with the play talking about unconnected things. Sighing deeply Nellie left the room and sat on the stairs. Apart from his good looks, this particular clergyman had considerable charm and a flashing smile which displayed large white teeth.

When he had gone, Nellie returned. She stumped crossly to the chair in which she always sat with her knees very wide apart and with her aureole of sparse hair looking like a halo round her head, and said disapprovingly, ' 'Orrible face. Quite 'orrible. Always smiling. Like Jesus.' This I found a conversation stopper. A few nights later she said, 'Are yer a Caffolic, Miss Gray?'

'No, Nellie,' I replied.

'Are yer Jewish, Miss Gray?' she asked.

'No, Nellie,' I said.

'Then what are yer?'

'Church of England.'

She nodded delightedly. 'Good! Good!' she exclaimed. 'Church of England people never talk about their religion.' And we went back again to endless discussions about her 'ladies' and 'gentlemen'.

When the play finished, Michael was asked to play Higgins in *My Fair Lady* in Australia for three months. Originally he had been asked to go out for eighteen months but *Boyd* made that impossible. Now he accepted for the three. Our finances were not too good just then, so I tried to let the cottage, and eventually succeeded, and I began writing *Murder in Mind* for a new publisher Macdonald and Jane. I had left Arthur Barker and my very dear first publisher Herbert Van Thal, as Arthur Barker had been taken over by Weidenfeld, and Bertie was having a difficult time. One of the most generous, warm-hearted men I have ever met, he had given me constant encouragement and was a good friend, and I missed him dreadfully. Fortunately for me – and for Michael – Bertie was taken on to head the literary side of his brother's agency and, until his retirement in the middle 'seventies, our close friendship had the added element of professional literary interest which was meat and drink to him.

After two months, Michael found an Australian director willing to employ us in Australian television in Shaw's *A Village Wooing*, so I set off happily to Melbourne to join him. When I arrived Michael was desperately thin, also ill with flu but still performing. I had seen Rex Harrison and later I saw Tony Britton in the part of Higgins and they were both excellent; so was Michael. This Australian cast were good by any standards and the show a tremendous success, but Michael was exhausted and I was glad to be with him. *Village Wooing* broke all existing appreciation figures for a play on Australian TV. When it finished we were asked by the British Council to perform for them in Hong Kong. So we did a double bill of *Village Wooing* and *A Marriage Has Been Arranged*, which we had last done in one of the Ellen Terry Memorial performances at Smallhythe, her last home on the edge of Romney Marsh. Now we were the first professionals to play Hong Kong's new City Centre Theatre. We went via Singapore, which I hadn't seen for twenty-eight years, and which delighted me as at that time it hadn't changed much; and returned to England via Bangkok and Athens.

At home, Michael did a deal for a new series of *Boyd*, and we were asked to open the Ashcroft Theatre in Croydon. We were also suddenly rung up by someone enquiring what we were doing about publicity in Berlin. Mystified, we said 'Nothing,' and the voice said crossly, 'Well, don't you think you should? You are booked to give a Shakespeare programme at the Berlin Festival in three weeks' time.' It transpired that MCA (The Music Corporation of America), who had been our agents until their collapse while we were in Hong Kong, had arranged this in their death throes and had forgotten to tell us! With typical kindness, Frank Hauser devised and rehearsed a Shakespeare programme for us, which we performed in the exquisite Oak Gallery in the Charlottenburg Palace. It was luckily a great success, and we found Berlin vibrant and much of it beautiful, except for the new hideous breeze-block Wall which snaked along even through the windows of intervening houses; grim, forbidding and aggressive.

The opening of the Ashcroft Theatre, though, was not a success. The theatre is just one part of an ambitious leisure complex with facilities for concerts, wrestling, restaurants, circuses and lectures. It was a great honour to be asked, but the play was a stinker and the growing pains of the theatre painful indeed. There was no dressing-room on stage level, the stage apron which was meant to rise and sink electrically didn't work, the acoustics were bad, the box office closed for an hour during what should be the rush hour for box offices, the stage doorkeeper worked office hours so that, when he was needed he had gone home, and the first night was a shambles.

Peggy Ashcroft, who had been born in Croydon and in whose honour the theatre had been built, started the proceedings by reciting a poem especially written for her by John Betjeman. She was followed by Andrew Cruickshank making a very long speech, and then our too long play started. Michael as an El Greco Henry VIII (he had not yet put back the weight he had lost in Australia) dressed in the basement, and Polly Adams, Gillian Raine and Pamela Ann Davey, among others, dressed in a communal dressing-room five floors up, next to my single cell. We were only allowed to use the lift if there was no concert next door. Needless to say there was one. Nothing went right but at least it wasn't quite as difficult as the third night, when a rather jolly all-in-wrestler asked me to go out and have a drink with him. I was in the middle of my performance as Catherine of Aragon, dressed from head to foot in black velvet with a huge stage diamond cross in my cleavage. I politely declined. He took no offence, but went next door to the girls' room. Pamela Ann, a beautiful Australian redhead, was just about to go on stage as Anne Boleyn when the wrestler repeated his invitation to her. She told him to get lost and he felled her with a karate chop. All this was twenty-eight years ago.

We have been to the Ashcroft once or twice since, but I can't say it's my favourite theatre, although things have much improved. I have a phobia about leisure complexes. Quite simply they give *me* a complex, although I did see one most astounding act in a Christmas circus there. An enormous handsome woman dressed in a tuxedo strolled about whistling the latest pop tune. On her head was a huge transparent pink plastic box. In it a blonde was stripping. The whistling woman had the biggest neck I've yet beheld.

ve: Left, as the Old Man and Old Woman in *The Chairs* in 1961; right, with Keith Baxter in *Where Angels*
 to Tread.
. Forster approved the adaptation and often visited my dressing-room. It was the start of a most
eeable correspondence.

w: Left, as Mrs Alving in *Ghosts*; and right, Mrs 'Candour and Sir Peter Teazle in *School for Scandal* at
dsor in 1971.

A very different Mrs Candour at the Duke of York's in 1984, after a quick change from playing Lady Snee

Dulcie Gray

It was extremely cold that Christmas time, but there was no room for the sea lions' tank indoors. During the night the water froze and, when the time came for them to do their act throwing balls to one another, their noses were so swollen and painful that they utterly refused. A baby elephant got claustrophobia in the lift and, once in the ring, refused to leave it, performing its act over and over again, rather than return via the lift, and Michael, again dressing in the basement, was suddenly aware of a loud slithering and thumping sound combined with a terrible smell, and opened his door to see the boxing kangaroo on its way to work.

23

Rather battered by our experience at Croydon, we decided to approach Glen Byam Shaw who, with Anthony Quayle, had run Stratford while Michael was there, before handing over to Peter Hall. We badly wanted to do a minor classic and, as Glen was now a freelance director, we asked him if he would direct us in *A Month in the Country*. He seemed delighted with the idea but was a little worried that the dates we suggested, which were dictated by the final series of *Boyd*, might conflict with a commitment he already had, to direct for Binkie. Then came a lovely surprise, would we like to be in Binkie's new play, an adaptation of E. M. Forster's novel *Where Angels Fear to Tread*? The parts we were offered, Caroline Abbot and Philip Heriton, were particularly rewarding. We just had time for a holiday, so we went to Italy, visiting Florence, Siena, Urbino, Assisi and San Gimignano – Forster country – in order to immerse ourselves in the places he was writing about.

It was an entirely satisfactory run in an entirely satisfactory play. Keith Baxter played the Italian boy superbly and, most fortunate of all, we saw quite a lot of Forster himself. He professed himself especially pleased with Keith and me, and sometimes came into my dressing-room at the St Martin's to talk. Caroline was based on his only heterosexual love and he seemed glad to talk about those early days. He had disliked his mother and his aunt – or at least had felt imprisoned and dominated by them and 'Caroline', and Italy, and Keith's character seemed to have freed him. He was less in sympathy with Michael's character, whom we took to be a portrait of his own young self. He seemed quite at ease in a dressing-room, and there were long, quite comfortable silences as I did my make-up. He was interested to know how I had set about portraying Caroline, because I had come so near to his vision. He said how much he loved Cambridge, 'where I am easy now in my own restrictions,' he said. 'I make my own rules.'

He wrote me a series of charming letters, of diminishing formality.

Dear Miss Gray and Company. Dear Miss Gray, Dear Dulcie Gray – Dear Dulcie – signed E. M. Forster – E. Morgan Forster – Morgan Forster and finally Morgan. A lovely man. A lovely time. We opened in Cambridge, had a few weeks at the Arts in London, ran for nine months at the St Martin's, then went on tour. Wonderful.

April 29th, 1964 was our Silver Wedding anniversary. Michael arranged a service at St Saviour's, Walton Street, where we had been married in 1939, with a lunch directly afterwards and a cocktail party the following evening for those who didn't feel religiously in-clined. It was fun seeing so many friendly theatrical faces in church on a happy occasion. Gatherings of actors in churches are usually for memorial services. At the cocktail party Binkie Beaumont started Jane Birkin's career by offering her a silent part in one of his plays.

1964 was the quatercentenary of Shakespeare's birth. Our own contribution was a recital which we called *Merely Players*, and was an expanded version of what we had done in Berlin. We took it to Rome, Geneva, Montreux, Rosehill, King's Lynn, the Bristol Old Vic and the beautifully restored Regency Theatre in Bury St Edmunds. The climax of the celebrations as far as the whole profession was concerned, though, was an afternoon tea party given by the Queen at Buckingham Palace. Her Majesty spent a lot of time with her guests, and put them so much at their ease that the formal hour of departure came and went unnoticed. Michael negotiated his next West End play, *Hostile Witness*, with Peter Saunders in the Blue Drawing-Room, and as the summer dusk began falling, the company at last began drifting away, some of them in the most unlikely collection of vehicles ever permitted to park within the palace gates. The Queen looked radiant. Her natural complexion was the loveliest I have ever seen.

Michael spent nearly a year in *Hostile Witness* at the Haymarket and I went to Birmingham to play Madam Arkadina in *The Seagull*. It was a very unhappy time which was doubly sad as it was a part I had always wanted to play. The play succeeded, but the cast was unfriendly; almost unique in my experience.

1965 saw Michael still acting in *Hostile Witness* and, in June, I had one of my favourite television engagements – *Beautiful For Ever*. It was the true story of Madame Rachelle, a fraudulent beautician who retailed Jordan Water from the tap. Though she lived in Victorian times, a preparation called Rachelle powder cream was still being sold in the 'thirties, and I remember secretly using it on my nose before I was allowed to use make-up. Ellen Pollock played Madame Rachelle, and I the most pathetic of her dupes.

We now began to work for one of the sweetest men who have ever graced the theatre – Peter Bridge. By this time Peter had had a string of West End successes to his credit, and we were already friends. He came to us with a plan for multi-star revivals which would tour the major cities and then come to town for limited seasons. He felt that a guaranteed London run and a firm stop date would neutralise any antipathy his distinguished casts might feel to touring. For us it sounded perfect. At the same time Peter Donald was desperate for productions for his chain of theatres and had had a complete change of heart about touring the classics. We put them in touch with one another.

Peter Bridge was just forty, but looked much younger. He was married to his beloved Roslyn and had three young boys. He had spent most of the 'fifties in a variety of front-of-house jobs in the West End, and for three years had been in charge of sport for Associated Rediffusion Television. His passion for the theatre was total. He loved actors, playwrights and directors, and seemed to have limitless energy. Between 1958 and 1970, he put on sixty productions – many of them box office successes and many artistically distinguished. He also discovered Alan Ayckbourn in Scarborough.

We all racked our brains for the right play to establish what became Allied Theatre Productions and I thought of Wilde's *An Ideal Husband*. In order to get it off the ground, Michael and I suggested that we should play the very dull Sir Robert and Lady Chiltern – a real self-sacrifice but worth it (just!), and Margaret Lockwood, Roger Livesey, his wife Ursula Jeans and Richard Todd made up a very sound cast. The production was the most enormous success. In spite of lavish sets and costumes Allied were in the black before the end of the tour and, in London, it soon became obvious (in spite of some fairly bad reviews) that ten to twelve weeks would be quite inadequate to accommodate the crowds who wanted to see it. The original plan had been that, once a play was settled into its West End house, we should start rehearsing the next. Almost no-one in the cast wanted to leave the play, however. A whopping commercial theatrical success comes only too rarely in many actors' lives. Michael and I therefore left on our own to start Allied's second venture, *On Approval* by Frederick Lonsdale, first on tour, then at the St Martin's Theatre. This had wonderful and meaty parts for us both and, as it has only a cast of four and two sets, it was not too expensive to mount. Robert Flemyng and Polly Adams played the two other parts, and Murray MacDonald, an old friend, was our director. A happier choice was not possible. The tour was a bumper one, and we opened splendidly in London, but the two Peters and we ourselves were still hankering after the original idea of repertoire in the West End and wanted a new play to alternate with *On Approval* at the St Martin's. (Repertoire means two or more plays alternating at the same theatre. Actors like it because they are not doing the same thing week in, week out. Why managers hanker after it is a mystery to me.) They found Giles Cooper's *Happy Family* and a fascinating play it is. For some reason the public hated it (and hated its recent revival) as much as actors and critics love it.

Giles had been at drama school with us, where as a shy fair-haired student who blushed if you talked to him, and bent his knees and shut his eyes while acting, we had been devoted to him but would hardly have predicted a great theatrical future for him. (In the days when we were all at drama school together, men were like gold. At the Webber Douglas as I have said there were seventy-five girls and seven men.) We never knew that his real intention was to be a writer. We had a very enthusiastic reunion up in Newcastle and looked forward with great excitement to starting work once *On Approval* had opened in town. Lovely Polly, though she happily remained in *On Approval*, didn't play the younger sister in *Happy Family*, but another dear friend Gillian Raine from *Candida* played it instead.

No sooner was all this arranged than there was a terrible tragedy. Giles had been having a celebratory dinner at the Garrick. On his way home in the train to his house in the country, he opened the carriage door and fell to his death. I don't believe it was suicide. Peter Bridge said that his usual train had a corridor on that side.

His widow wanted us to go on with the play. Gillian's performance was so good that she got an award, but nothing could save it. What's more, it knocked out the success of *On Approval* which was playing alternate weeks.

We went back on the road with *On Approval* and, staying at the Grand Hotel in Manchester, we were asked by our table waiter if we could get Vivien Leigh's autograph. I wrote to her and Vivien sent him one at once. She also sent us a very affectionate postcard in an extremely shaky handwriting saying how happy she was that things were going so well with us and our marriage. Considering that her own marriage was over, and that at that time she was both ill and unhappy, it was wonderfully generous. Typically so. She died two days later.

The books about Vivien, dwelling on her depressions and difficulties, only tell one half of her story. She could be wonderful. What is more, she could be a wonderful actress. Her professional dedication was total: she was a star of the first magnitude in films, and although not always happily cast in the theatre – who is? – gave a number of radiant and unforgettable performances. Her Cleopatras carried all before her – the critics too. Ivor Brown in *The Observer* called her 'A lass unparalleled'. *The Skin of Our Teeth, The Doctor's Dilemma* and *The School for Scandal* were other notable successes. Larry, talking about her performance in *Streetcar*, said in *Confessions*, 'I thought if the critics have one grain of fairness they will give her credit now for being an actress, and not go on for ever letting their judgements be distorted by her great beauty and her Hollywood stardom!'

Alas, led by Ken Tynan, they never really did.

Tynan implied that later they became enormous friends. Rachel Kempson and her husband, Michael Redgrave, who were almost Vivien's greatest friends, saw no sign of it and Rachel says that frankly she doesn't believe it. She says that Ken Tynan boasted to Victor Stiebel that he would split the Oliviers. Vivien was no fool and she loved Larry.

24

I was writing *The Murder of Love* that year – a novel I am quite glad I have written as, although it is a grim sort of book, my psychiatrist friend, Dr Tredgold from University College Hospital, said it is the best portrayal of a psychopathic killer he has ever read in a novel. Perhaps that was because I used a great deal of what he told me!

When I started writing, I had headed for a kind of sub-Agatha Christie approach (I read her books on holidays and enjoyed their expertise). Gradually I became interested in crime itself and read a great deal about it. Why-dunnit then became more important to me than who-dunnit. Motive must surely fascinate any writer, and murder is the extreme crime. Bertie Van Thal then asked me to write stories for his *Pan Book of Horror Stories* series, and I found they came easily. Crime writers have always seemed to me to be gentler than most other people, and horror story writers gentler still (though of course this is a generalisation). I am easily frightened, and so can easily conjure up what frightens me. In fact I dislike writing horror stories. Not so crime.

For my crime novels, I also went to the police; Scotland Yard was very helpful and, for some time, a Lieutenant-Colonel C. H. Farthing, Ex-Superintendent of the Metropolitan Police Force, was also wonderfully kind and helpful. Chemists were also very supportive.

One day we had a new au-pair girl arriving. I had to go out before meeting her, so I left her a note asking her to do some shopping at the local shops. I made a list of what I wanted, including fresh vegetables and aspirin, and added 'and please ask the chemist the amount required for a fatal dose of strychnine'.

Fortunately Michael found the note before she went on her errand, and explained why I wanted to know!

The Murder of Love was written at just about the time of the abolition of capital punishment, and although finally it didn't influence the book, I managed to get hold of a copy of the debates in Hansard which make absorbing reading.

During the final months and the beginning of the next year, we were both in Ronald Millar's *No. 10* with Alistair Sim and John Gregson. We opened in Scotland, then flew to Toronto for English Fortnight, playing in the 3,500-seater O'Keefe Centre. The building was far too large for us (or for any play) but we had a marvellous time and then we went to Montreal for two days to see the British stand at Expo '67, after which we resumed our British tour in Golders Green! The tour went well, but once we reached the Strand in London, it was downhill all the way. We ran for a few months, but never to really good houses.

We holidayed in Morocco and stayed at the Mamounia Hotel in the room which had been Churchill's during the war. The windows looked out on the lovely gardens and the Atlas mountains. To one side of the hotel was a huge dusty expanse, on which hundreds of Bedouin tents were pitched. The biggest tents were very large and furnished with rich carpets and silver lamps and tableware. The tiniest tents had tin equivalents imported from Manchester. By day the tribesmen galloped their magnificent horses, twenty or thirty abreast, until within a few yards of their Chieftains, then reined in so fiercely to a halt that their mounts reared up. As they did so the riders fired their rifles single-handedly into the air. This performance, repeated tribe by tribe, was called a fantasia. The next morning they were gone without trace; not a scrap of paper, no tin cans or bottles or any litter of any kind. Not like our own dear countrymen in any way at all!

At the end of our stay, we visited Field Marshal Sir Claude Auchinleck on an introduction by Edward Seago, who was encouraging Michael to paint. Sir Claude, who had also been tutored in painting by Ted Seago, was surrounded by his own pictures, sharply focused little landscapes in water colour and, when we arrived, he was listening to an Australian Test-match commentary. He lived alone in a poky little flat with one Arab servant. He was a beautiful man, big with a craggy face, masses of white hair and a lean figure. He spoke with deep affection of the Indian Army in which he had served from 1903 to 1947, and said that his best years were when he commanded his battalion – the 1st Punjabis. He begged us to drive through the Atlas mountains with him into the Sahara. But we could not, as it was time for us to go home.

We returned in time for Michael to do Joe Orton's *Funeral Games* for television with Vivien Merchant, Bill Fraser and Ian MacShane. When it was shown in Monaco, the hierarchy was so shocked that they banned it from their film festival and the stars were also, for the time being, banned from the principality. After this untoward piece of notoriety for Michael, we went to Nottingham to do an interesting and original modern play by Maisie Mosco called *Vacant Possession*, and an unwieldy and unlikely play by Arbuzov who had had a great success with *The Promise*.

The Russians sent up a posse from their Embassy to see this last and were very suspicious of the fact that I wore a red wig. 'Why?' they kept on saying. 'What is the significance? Redheads only come from Georgia' (or don't come from Georgia, I have forgotten now which). As I had only decided to wear a red wig because the play, the clothes and the set were so drab that I thought the audience needed something to enliven them, I was unable to supply a satisfactory answer.

One night a disgruntled young man in the cast, who had been given a small part and squeaking shoes, decided to do a little enlivening of his own. He hung a bright green rubber fluorescent spider just six inches above where the hero of the play would be sleeping in his prison cell. He handed a carefully made crimson satin penis with bells on it to my stage husband in lieu of a gun, and a box, heavily labelled 'The Pill', to me, instead of ammunition.

This was on our last night in Nottingham. I don't know what happened to the young man. I believe he became a writer. In fact the whole season was rather depressing. John Neville, who had been a much-loved artistic director, had quarrelled with his overlords on the local authority and had resigned before a successor was chosen. Half the company were so loyal to him that they either left or wanted to leave, and the rest felt guilty about wanting to stay on.

Fortunately for us, our next job was very different, though it too certainly had its hazards. John Roberts, who had been Brian Brooke's second in command in South Africa, offered us a play which in America had been called *Absence of a Cello*, and in England was entitled *Out of the Question*. It was a slightly pretentious comedy, which had not succeeded in America but which, with some changes, had done very well in France. Nigel Patrick directed and Gladys Cooper, then aged seventy-nine, co-starred with us.

Gladys was adorable. A great and famous beauty in her youth and one of the few women theatre managers ever, she still had immense glamour and a wicked sense of humour. She was mad about dogs and Titus, our white labrador, was a great favourite. She dressed beautifully, was very slim, had large brilliant blue eyes and thin expressive hands. She was well-known for not knowing her lines, but was delightfully easy to work with.

Our programme proclaimed that 'Dame Gladys' socks were by Marks and Spencer'! She objected forcefully. Her personal wardrobe consisted entirely of couture clothes, and she saw no reason to wear cheap clothes in the play. Why she wore socks at all at the start of the tour, I don't know. She didn't later!

Although much older than the rest of us, she was the pivot and lodestar of the company. She disliked talking about the past, except about her first part in *Bluebell in Fairyland* and her association (business only, she insisted) with Gerald du Maurier when she was at the Playhouse, but she was always interested in the future. On matinée days old ladies by the dozen made their adoring way to the dressing-room after the show. If they looked their age (she didn't look hers) and then asked her to help them down the stairs from her room after the visit, having said that they had been her fans since their childhoods, she was outraged and came to tell us about it.

When forbidden to drive herself back to Henley after the show, she hired a firm of two handsome young brothers, who drove her back in a Lotus Elan which could do 120 mph.

I played an English academic, but Ira Wallach, the author, wanted me to make my part more cosy. This was surprisingly silly considering he had written a far more interesting character, and, when I told him that I would rather model her on my own Aunt Gemma at Oxford, he said that I had no experience of academics and became very upset. The money from the play was American and the Americans then ganged up on me and wanted me removed. John Roberts, Nigel Patrick, Gladys and Michael all said they would leave if I went. Once we reached London, however, all was very well and we ran until Gladys, Michael and I left of our own accord nearly a year later.

Gladys had her eightieth birthday during the run, and John Roberts, the kindest of men, decided to give her a party she would never forget. We were playing to capacity houses at the St Martin's and, on the night of her birthday, he came to our dressing-room just before the show to tell us that we had an invited audience in front and so we were not to be worried if the laughter and applause were not very loud. It was lucky that he told us because we did indeed notice a difference and Gladys, who had not been told, was deeply shocked. More was to come. In the play, when the grandson had to open the door to a friend, it was Robert Morley, Gladys's son-in-law, who entered instead, carrying a bottle of champagne and some glasses. He handed a full glass to the surprised and disapproving Gladys, who drank hers, half toasting what she thought was a paying audience.

Robert gave us all a drink, then he went to the edge of the stage and said words to the effect of 'Ladies and gentlemen, as you know, tonight we are celebrating the eightieth birthday of a remarkable and wonderful woman, Gladys Cooper.' Then he turned to Gladys. 'The house has been bought out. Eighty of your friends are in front. The play will now stop and we'll all go across the road to the Ivy and have dinner. Thank you so much everyone.' And the audience stood up and cheered.

With her blue eyes flashing, Gladys said to me in a low voice, 'But I'm on percentage!'

At supper I found myself next to Lewis Casson – now in his nineties, nearly blind, deaf, short, stocky and sitting bolt upright. He and I were very good friends and, of course, everyone loved Sybil Thorndyke, his beloved wife. Suddenly Lewis said, 'Dulcie, I have suddenly become very preoccupied with the question of eternity. Do you think, if Sybil and Michael don't mind, that you and I could have lunch together one day so that we can discuss it?' Alas he died before the lunch could be arranged.

We had met Sybil and Lewis at a splendid supper at the Savoy one night some years before, after a performance of *The Three Sisters* by Lee Strasberg's Studio Company of New York, and had become devoted to them. At the same table that night were Frankie Howerd who became a great friend too, David Warner, and James Baldwin, who said he always made a point of watching my films on American television. I frankly didn't believe him, but he described them all minutely. The meal was superb and, with great satisfaction, Sybil boomed across to Lewis, 'Better than cocoa and biscuits, isn't it, darling?'

Michael was an usher at Lewis's memorial service at Westminster Abbey the following year. Memorial services vary unexpectedly. Binkie and Noël were to die within a week of each other. Binkie, who was really known by comparatively few, had an intimate and revealing service. Noël's was disappointing and strangely impersonal for someone who could number his friends in hundreds. The later service, when a plaque was unveiled for him in Westminster Abbey, went a long way to making up for this. Queen Elizabeth the Queen Mother, a small figure in purple velvet and a great admirer of Noël, was present as an orchestra played his music, including 'I'll See You Again'. The acoustics of the Abbey made it not only lovely but, for those of us who loved him, heartbreaking.

We have so many happy and hospitable memories of Noël. He came to lunch with us at Cumberland Place in 1968, and told us that Gertrude Lawrence had once lived in our house and, in the following year, on his seventieth birthday, we performed in the midnight Gala at the Phoenix in which every word and note of music was his. He was knighted in the New Year Honours, and invited us with 'just family' as he called it, to celebrate it at the Savoy. 'Just family' was a huge party, but it wasn't an affectation of Noël's to call it family. He had a small inner caucus of friends who were with him most of the time, and then this other great circle of loving and loved people, whom he managed to make a part of his life. *A Talent to Amuse* he certainly had, but 'A Talent for Friendship' was another of his special gifts.

25

In the 'sixties, Michael and I had eight joint appearances in the West End, and success in seven. A lucky decade. The 'seventies were a roller coaster decade. They began very happily with *Three*, a Shaw triple bill at the Fortune with Bobbie Flemyng, a great friend since *On Approval*, June Barry, whom Michael had met on *Boyd*, and the young Clive Francis, already marvellously versatile and soon to become a brilliant portrait cartoonist. A better cast couldn't have been possible. The first play was *How He Lied* with Bobbie, June and Clive, and Michael directing. *Village Wooing* by now directed itself (we had done it on and off all over the world) and *Press Cuttings* was directed by Ray Cooney, fresh from acting in farce at the Whitehall, whose protean energy includes writing, acting and founding the renowned Theatre of Comedy Company. *Press Cuttings* is a rarity and, with judicious cutting by Michael, was extremely funny. Set in the period of the suffragettes, I played a Gorgon of a woman who believed that all great men were really women in drag, and Michael a feeble Cabinet Minister, also in drag. It was a joyful play to do, and was liked by the critics.

Some actors say they don't read their notices. I can't think why. A good critic, and there are many, knows a great deal about the theatre and can be enormously helpful to actors by providing standards that could easily be lowered without his well-informed views. Some actors only read the notices when the play is over, because they feel they may be too depressed by bad ones or too elated by good ones. This has logic but it wouldn't do for me. Critics and actors rarely meet. They feel they are on two different sides of the theatre. Of the very few critics I have known personally, most have become friends.

And so to *The Wild Duck*, our next play for Glen Byam Shaw. Of all the directors I have worked with so far, I think he has been my favourite. He had authority, taste and a passion for what he was doing that engendered total trust. He was exquisite to look at, with his silvery hair and his blue eyes, pink cheeks and tall lean figure. He spoke in a very very soft voice, which sometimes became a little strangulated, and he was wonderfully affectionate. I wish he hadn't died.

He was given no memorial service, which in a way was typical. Although he ran Stratford with Tony Quayle, Tony was knighted. Glen was not, and this in spite of his magnificent work later at the English National Opera. Perhaps he had asked for no memorial service. He was an intensely private person. So on October 5th, 1986 we asked his family and some of his friends to a private memorial lunch at home. John Gielgud, Peggy Ashcroft, Rachel Kempson and Meriel Forbes (the widows of Michael Redgrave and Ralph Richardson), 'Percy' Harris and Elizabeth Montgomery (the survivors of the 'Motley' trio, his favourite designers), Marius Goring and Eddie Kulukundis were there to toast his memory. Tony Quayle, Johnnie Mills, Emlyn Williams and Wendy Hiller sent messages as they were all working! Larry was ill.

To go back to *The Wild Duck*.

Hayley Mills played Hedvig. It was her first West End play, after all those enchanting child film performances and, like her sister Juliet, she was a natural. The tour was a triumph – for Hayley really – but things went wrong at the Criterion and the play failed.

The failure in London may have been partly due to the fact that we had to have a paid lay-off for some weeks between the tour and London, because no West End theatre was available. Somehow the play had lost its impetus when we reconvened. The critics didn't seem to like Hayley's performance so much in London. From where we were I thought it magical, but the play really depended on her. It was a time when to some people, starring in films disqualified you from being taken seriously in the theatre. It was all right for established theatre actors like Olivier, Finney or Maggie Smith to branch out into films. But established film stars who attempted only occasionally to make forays the other way across the divide did so at their peril.

At Brighton just before we came to town, I had a funny dressing-room encounter which afterwards assumed great poignancy. Larry Olivier came through to my dressing-room after a matinée to tell me he had liked my performance. We got talking and I asked him what he was doing.

'*Guys and Dolls*, I hope,' he said, 'but I've got this bloody thrombosis thing, phlebitis.'

'What's phlebitis?' I asked.

'Look,' said Larry, and he dropped his trousers round his ankles.

He was perfectly respectable in a bright blue Y-front, but at that moment an old lady knocked at my door. I called out 'Just a minute'. However she was deaf so she walked in.

Larry was quite unperturbed, but she and I were both somewhat thrown.

'Do you know Lord Olivier?' sounded strange in the circumstances.

The sad thing was that really from then on Larry was struggling with one illness after another, and he never did do *Guys and Dolls*. He was as brave as a lion, and a great fighter, but what a struggle he had to keep going!

Early the following year, Michael and I went back to Malaya. Michael was writing a book about us, and wanted to see Kuala Lumpur and Fraser's Hill.

Kuala Lumpur airport then was the only building in concrete I have ever admired (what a muddy and aggressive material concrete usually is!). It had turrets and domes and charm. Sadly it has been pulled down, and the usual grim air-travel wilderness substituted. Kuala Lumpur itself was only just embarking on high-rise nightmares and, behind the new museum, we actually found 'itou black Uncle', the dark green bust of Edward VII that I used to kiss on the way to the 'padang' to play when I was a little girl. It was lying derelict on the grass.

Fraser's Hill too was almost unchanged. The school had become an American Methodist holiday home, and its red corrugated iron roof had been painted green. The little bathrooms had been updated, but otherwise it was the same as when I was there. There was even the bed with the walnut-finish bedhead I had slept in at the time of my struggle with the scorpion.

For some strange reason, a sort of gazebo had been built over the start of the jungle path which led to the golf course, but the wah-wah monkeys were still leaping from tree to tree above the white mists in the early morning, the golf course was still in existence, with its sad millipedes, and a rather nasty new Chinese hotel had risen where the golf shop had been, and some imported London street lamps lined the drive of a rich man's house.

It was a wonderful trip; and I felt utterly at home, but when we arrived back in England we found that Titus, by now sixteen years old, was dying. He had just managed to struggle through until he saw us. The vet came and we buried him in the park near our new home in Amersham. We were tired and jet-lagged, and it was a terrible shock and a great unhappiness. He was a beautiful dog, both in looks and in nature.

The following day Eileen, our housekeeper, Michael and I all went at different times to see his grave. Desolate, I offered up a little prayer that I could have some sign that he was all right. It was totally ridiculous, and I knew it was, but I was knocked out. Nothing happened. No dog in the vicinity barked. No heavenly music sounded. No vision of the old boy appeared, and I went indoors to occupy my hands and my mind with the move we were making from one flat to another in the big house we had now decided to make our permanent home in the country. We had moved a great deal of furniture from Regent's Park into the drawing-room of the new flat. Pictures were stacked along one wall, books along another, kitchen utensils, china, lamps, ornaments and small things were placed at both ends of the room, and in the middle, rising to about nine feet, was a mass of furniture. As we walked into the room that morning, the wooden floor must have moved, and a book was dislodged from the summit of the pile. The book fell to the floor, spine upwards. Michael picked it up. It was an engagement diary for 1955, Michael's Stratford years, where we had bought Titus. There were two entries – Wednesday: *Titus Andronicus* opens. Friday: Titus the puppy arrives. I'd had my sign.

After a long and arduous tour of *The Clandestine Marriage* and the collapse at the eleventh hour of a West End play for which we had been contracted, it was a very special pleasure to be involved in a joyful production of *School for Scandal* directed by David Conville at Windsor, with Gabrielle Drake as a lovely Lady Teazle, Michael an excellent Sir Peter and me as Mrs Candour.

The following year, we tried out a new play called *The Dragon Variation*, also at Windsor. Michael then played Prospero in *The Tempest* in Regent's Park, directed by our good and clever friend Richard Digby Day (Wayne Sleep was a magical Ariel), and we bought a yellow labrador puppy whom we called Prospero. I went on a tour of *Hay Fever* for Duncan Weldon – now a friend and the most prolific of West End managers. Noël rang me to wish me good luck and, for the first time in my life I didn't recognise him, he sounded so ill. It was the last time I ever heard his voice. Typical of Noël to think of his friends, even when ill! When he had also been very ill some years before, just as we were about to open in *On Approval*, we had a first night telegram from him from America. He had just struggled through a terrible time, and was staying with the Lunts.

Above: Our beloved Titus appeared with us in *Let Them Eat Cake*, but he did not enjoy acting and had to have arrowroot biscuits after each performance to calm his nerves.

Below: Noël Coward had an enormous talent for friendship.

Above: Michael's adaptation of Pinero's *The Cabinet Minister*. From the left, Michael, Dulcie, Evelyn Laye, Brian Carroll, Judith Arthy, Susie Blake, Martin Potter.

Below: An informal moment with Ingrid Bergman; left, as Miss Marple. While rehearsing for the tour of *A Murder is Announced* I learnt that *Butterflies on my Mind* had won an award.

We then went on a tour of *The Dragon Variation*. Goodness, that play! It was maddening! It was never really right, but had so many good ideas that we kept on trying. It also had a wonderful part for Michael, and when Duncan asked us to tour yet again, with a view to going into London, we foolishly agreed. Our last job of the year was *Alice Through the Looking Glass* at the dreaded Ashcroft Theatre, Croydon.

In the spring Michael Codron asked us to do *Absurd Person Singular*, but we felt ourselves in honour bound to stay with Duncan although we had as yet no contracts; and, in fact, we did resume *The Dragon Variation*, this time directed by Richard Digby Day. At the Richmond theatre, I was caught for *This is Your Life*. Michael had had a very difficult time keeping it secret, but to my amazement I thoroughly enjoyed it. They found Jane Boulenger, Joyce and Jeremy Green with whom I had come back from Malaya, June Reeve-Tucker, one of my ex-pupils, Barbara Mullen, Hayley Mills, Tito Gobbi and James Mason (on film), Totie (on film) and Dickie Attenborough in person from his home across the Green, so it was a very happy gathering.

The Dragon Variation toured and toured, but didn't get to London. Noël died – and Binkie too – and we were out of work. A wretched, and sad time.

Blessedly soon, however, Ray Cooney and John Gale offered us a very funny play by William Douglas Home called *At the End of the Day*. It was a political comedy about 10 Downing Street. Johnnie Mills played a spoof Harold Wilson character. I was his loyal wife Mabel, and Michael was his Ted Heath-type opponent. We toured and went into the Savoy, where we ran for nearly a year.

Working with Johnnie was a joy. He is now in his eighties and looks twenty years younger, then he was just seventy and looked fifty with his bright blue eyes, great sense of humour, trim figure and infectious laugh. He has had an astonishing career. He started in the back row of the chorus in *The Five O'Clock Girl* at the London Hippodrome and became a musical star and then a straight theatre star within a few years. He is a film star with over a hundred films behind him, heaven knows how many theatre and television plays he has done, and he has won many many awards. He's frankly adorable. Mary, his wife, was acting as his dresser. She's a great girl, totally loyal, a splendid home-maker and a wonderful friend. She's also a very good writer. Their son Jonathan takes after her. He, too, has red hair, and is now making a name for himself as a script writer in Hollywood. All in all, doing *At the End of the Day* was a happy time.

Michael began 1975 as a token white Pooh Bah in a brilliant production, *The Black Mikado*. The otherwise all black cast were multi-talented, and Braham Murray directed with tremendous flair. At the end of the show on the London first night, the audience danced in the aisles! We still see Floella Benjamin, Patti Boulaye and Vernon Nesbith, and were devoted to the whole cast.

Michael modelled his Pooh Bah on Harold Macmillan, who came round after the show one night before Michael had had time to take off his make-up. They looked remarkably alike and Macmillan, who had loved the show, was highly delighted.

'Do you ever take a holiday?' he asked. 'If so, I'll come and take over.'

His family and friends saw it again several times. Michael was thirty years older than the next oldest in that cast, and danced and sang with the best of them. Rebecca West wrote him this brilliant notice.

'Dear Michael,

I was watching you last night and enjoying every minute of it. I marvelled that Whitey could keep up with the Niagara flow of African energy, and Whitey certainly did, though I quaked to think what the two matinée days must be like. I loved your Macmillan look and voice . . . What miracles they are, miracles of loveliness, miracles of skill, miracles of grotesqueness, and what *industry*, what perfectionist passion there is behind it. The Mikado has the presence of Chaliapin, he roars for all the bull bisons that were created. And that Tit Willow song is marvellous, so absolutely right and ungreasy, if you know what I mean.'

And then as a postscript –

'What a chancy business yours is. There you are in that unlikely milieu doing a lovely piece of work, part of a lovely whole. I saw Paul Schofield the other day playing Prospero – the island being converted into a drill hall; and Ariel standing in the gallery wearing tight pants and looking like a caretaker. I suppose Paul Schofield, like myself, could never have thought that any production of *The Tempest* could work out that way – any way his spirit died.'

How lucky Michael and I were to have Rebecca's friendship which had so surprisingly dated from her praise of my book *Baby Face*! Alas, we only knew her in the last twenty years of her life, but she was a constant joy; always interested, a brilliant conversationalist, and she fitted in with every type of company. She loved actors and the theatre. She had after all trained at RADA, and briefly became a professional actress. Her choice of language was wonderfully precise. Her rather actressy voice ornamented the stories she chose to tell perfectly. Among our friends she particularly liked Dick and Mary Francis, and Frankie Howerd. The animosity of her son made her extremely unhappy. 'He blames me for not marrying H. G. [Wells],' she said despairingly, 'which is macabre, when for many years marrying him was all I wanted in life!' She gave a very amusing party the last Christmas of her life, for Jilly and Leo Cooper and Michael and me, and there was no age-gap among any of us. There never was until her last year, when she suddenly seemed very old indeed – still lamenting the quarrels between herself and her son. When she had a bad fall in the autumn, she sent for Michael and gave him a lovely aquamarine and diamond brooch for me, and then a few weeks later she literally turned her face to the wall to die. She was eighty-nine.

Michael read at her memorial service. Bernard Levin did the eulogy. When we went out of the church into the daylight, a man detached himself from one of the pillars.

'May I join you for lunch?' he asked.

He was Wells's legitimate son, a professor at Reading. I thought how pleased Rebecca would have been that he was at the service.

Though I was working, I had a second bout of depression around this time. Noël Coward once waved his forefinger in my face and said firmly, 'Ena Spain is a bore.' (She was the ex-queen of Spain!) So are bouts of depression. Writing saved me. I was writing my sixteenth book, *Ride on a Tiger*, at this time.

My penultimate job that year was a short tour, beginning at the Festival Hall, of *Façade* with Gordon Jackson and Joe Melia. Both rehearsals and tour were too short, but what a fascinating engagement!

Alas, we never met Edith Sitwell, but met Sacheverell several times, as at one time he and Michael shared the same wine merchants, Hedges and Butler. 'Sash' called Michael 'Cousin' as his mother's family name was Denison – spelt the same way.

Façade is enormously difficult and complicated to perform. Fitting those words to that music is an intricate business. The music has its own unalterable rhythm, and music is more immediately accessible to an audience than words. I bought and endlessly played the Peter Pears/Sitwell recordings, and tried to reproduce Edith's rhythms and to match her relish exactly. It is, I think, the only way to do justice to the piece. An extraordinary coincidence occurred. Eileen, our housekeeper, was in America on holiday and we had advertised for someone to take her place. A charming woman, a Mrs Pears, came to us. She heard my rehearsals through the door, and said, 'Peter Pears is my ex-brother-in-law!'

The Festival Hall is not an easy place in which to perform, but in some ways it was a good choice for *Façade*, except that, surprisingly, the acoustics are not perfect, but it has a more intellectual connotation than that of a theatre, which is right. Even then, in 1976, it produced a violent reaction. We used no megaphones or screens, as they had in the hectically received first production, but people were either enchanted by Edith's wit and William Walton's brilliant interpretation of it, or insulted because they believed it to be a kind of hoax that they neither understood nor appreciated. So it was still ahead of its time. Now it would have complete acceptance, I think.

My year ended with a production of *Time and the Conways* at Guildford. In it were two splendidly clever young men; both of them had star quality, both were extremely attractive and both were very talented actors. One or other took the trouble to take me home every night. I have never ceased to be grateful to them, to admire them, and love them. Their names were Anthony Andrews and Christopher Cazenove. (The billing is alphabetical.)

26

Next summer Michael was touring with Anna Neagle, whom he loved, and I toured in *Ladies in Retirement* with the magical, ever beautiful and indomitable Evelyn Laye. To our horror she and I had to share a dressing-room in Peterborough, something that hadn't happened to Boo for fifty years of stardom. I was expecting her to be very angry, but of course she wasn't. There is far too much rubbish talked about bitchy actresses with outsize egos and blazing temperaments. I've met a few and very regrettable they are, or were – I think there were more about when I was starting – but it must be remembered that acting puts people under a lot of strain, and strain leads to temperaments. It was not at all unusual then for a dress rehearsal to last all night and be resumed almost until the opening of the show, with last-minute clothes fittings as well. Actors were dead tired and nervous. Not unnaturally. But this week in Peterborough was not our first week. Boo has probably got a temper; perhaps even a bad one (I certainly have), and a mercurial temperament is no bad thing in acting, but we knew each other reasonably well by this time and in the event we had enormous fun. We called each other 'matey' and laughed our heads off. Clement Freud's adorable wife Jill was also in the cast.

In the autumn Michael was asked to play Mr Barrett in Ronnie Millar's musical *Robert and Elizabeth*, adapted from *The Barretts of Wimpole Street* with Jeremy Brett (our Marchbanks at Oxford) as Browning, and Sally Ann Howes (who, as a teenager, had tested for *My Brother Jonathan*) as Elizabeth Barrett. The production was planned for a tour of Canada and Michael only agreed to the part if I could go with him. Duncan Weldon generously agreed.

Theatrical camp-following can be boring and awkward, partly because it means the camp follower, being out of work, is a sort of untouchable, partly too because all companies become tightly knit units very quickly. They have one aim in life – to make the play as good as possible. Everyone outside the unit is an interloper.

While they were still on tour at Guildford before going to Canada,

Michael's *This is Your Life* was done. Ronnie Millar lured him to lunch at the Inn on the Park, from where Michael at once wanted to go home as a heavy cold was threatening to smother him. Ronnie had enormous difficulty in keeping him long enough for Eamonn to catch him with the red book. In the end, Michael too enjoyed the experience.

At this time I had just begun writing my book on British butterflies, *Butterflies on my Mind*. The commission for it had come about in a very extraordinary way. When I was writing my crime books, I joined the Crime Writers' Association. A pleasanter collection of people than crime writers it would be difficult to meet. They are all clever, all seem to be outgoing, and all are gentle. Once a year they have a very good dinner. At one of these dinners, a man came up and asked me if I would do a book for his publishing company, that was not a crime story. I told him that I had always wanted to write a book on the conservation of British butterflies. He blanched a little and disappeared. The following year he came up to me again and said he would like me to write the book. As it was something I very much wanted to do, I rang Bertie Van Thal the following day and said 'Accept almost any offer if it's about the butterfly book.' He agreed.

Ian Dear from Angus and Robertson rang him the next morning and we fixed up a contract. My illustrator, Brian Hargreaves, was a young Yorkshireman who did a first-class job. We got on extremely well from the start, and he and his talented wife, Joyce, became good friends. In due course, the printers in Aylesbury gave a lunch party for me. Some local press were there, and one man asked how the book had come about. I told him the story and Ian Dear said, 'How extraordinary! I wasn't at the Crime Writers' Dinner.'

'Then how did you come into it?' I asked, and he said he had simply looked me up in *Who's Who*, had seen that I had put as my recreations swimming and butterflies, and had got on to Bertie! I never did discover who had approached me at the Crime Writers' Dinner.

I wasn't very keen on leaving Britain when I was in the middle of my butterfly research, but went with Michael to Canada, which anyway is a country I love whether I'm camp-following or not. It was very cold indeed in Ottawa where Michael was to open, and the snow was about eight feet deep. Michael went off to rehearse on the first morning, and I idly rang up the local library to ask if they had any books on British butterflies. They suggested I should contact the Experiment Farm, who replied that they had the best library of British butterflies outside the Natural History Museum. I went along to see them and I found everything I could possibly have wanted. I also discovered the almost pure joy of research. Day after day in blissful silence, I read the books I wanted and made my notes. One nugget I found that both pleased and distressed me. Mary Russell Mitford, a contemporary of Jane Austen, wrote about her in a letter to her niece describing her as the 'prettiest, silliest, most affected, husband-hunting butterfly' she ever remembered. In later years she described her as 'perpendicular, precise and taciturn'. I am a passionate fan of Jane Austen, and although Mrs Russell Mitford paints a vivid picture, it is also a very sad one.

I also discovered the word for butterfly in one of the northern Nigerian languages is *mallam-bude-talifa* which means *wise-man-open-the-book*.

On the opening night, I was in our hotel bedroom, having got myself dressed up for the occasion, when the telephone bell rang. A man's voice asked me if I were going to the theatre. I said I was, and he said he was going to see Sally Ann Howes and suggested we should have a drink together and then he'd take me to the theatre. I agreed and found him absolutely charming. *Robert and Elizabeth* then moved to Hamilton where, on the opening night, my new friend repeated his invitation and, in Toronto, the same thing happened. We found it very easy to talk to one another, and he knew about my writing and asked about my agent. I said Bertie was retiring, and he said *he* was a literary agent and now he is mine. It was extremely lucky for me. He is Douglas Rae, and Sally Ann Howes is his wife.

The tour of *Robert and Elizabeth* ended in Toronto and, before returning to England, we flew on to Bermuda to see Terence Rattigan who was dying of cancer. Michael had been his fag at Harrow and he had kept in friendly touch with us over the years, in bad times as well as good. So we went to say goodbye. He was being most lovingly cared for by Harold French (who had directed *My Brother Jonathan*) and his wife Peggy. We had dinner with Terry and, although he was often in quite terrible pain, he was in great form, full of plans for the future. His latest play was based on the notorious Rattenbury murder case. He wondered whether or not to call it *Cause Célèbre*, as pressure was being put on him to change the title. For what it was worth, we thought it a good title. He kept it. *Cause Célèbre* was a great success in London, and he was able to attend the opening before he died. He was also discussing other plays he wanted to write with a background of fact, either historical or contemporary. He asked us back the following evening, but was too ill to join us. It was wonderful for Terry to have such a success before he died. Both he and Noël had suffered terribly from the 'Osborne revolution', and both thought their careers were over. Noël triumphed with his cabaret at the Café de Paris (we were at the very exciting first night), then at Las Vegas, and from then on was back in business. Terry's theatrical recovery took longer – but he finished triumphantly.

We came back to do Michael's version of Pinero's *The Cabinet Minister* with Boo Laye and Pat Kirkwood among others, and with Duncan presenting. It went well everywhere but unfortunately didn't quite make it to the West End. Veronica and Gerald Flint Shipman, who ran the Phoenix, wanted it, but they were already contracted to do another play.

At that moment Peter Saunders offered me Miss Marple in *A Murder is Announced*. Agatha Christie is a phenomenon all on her own. She is an almost certain money-spinner and her fans, as well as being legion, are from every walk of life (Ladybird Johnson is one) and students wanted to do theses on me because of her.

I read all the Miss Marple books before I played her and was interested to find that she had begun almost mousily but, in the end, in her own way was quite a formidable woman with a wry sense of humour and the knitting was less in evidence. I met Dame Agatha only once at a party given for *The Mousetrap*, but she seemed very shy and we only had a few words.

This is a true story to illustrate her hold over audiences. A friend of mine was playing in an Agatha Christie in rep. As the curtain went up on Act I, there was the sound of a shot in the garden, called for in the script. The girl on stage, looking out of the window on the first night, was so nervous that instead of saying 'My God, Mary has been shot!' or words to that effect, said 'My God, so-and-so has shot Mary!' which was the entire plot of the play. The audience however still sat happily all through the evening trying to guess the identity of the murderer!

Our play was a great success and ran for a year at the Vaudeville, after which I went on tour with it. I enjoyed playing Miss Marple enormously, and loved working for Peter Saunders.

Michael kept busy playing Malvolio in *Twelfth Night*, Lebedov in *Ivanov*, and the Mayor in *The Lady's Not for Burning* for Toby Robertson's Prospect Company at the Old Vic. Sadly, Prospect disintegrated later, after a decade of distinguished touring of the classics, and, ironically, a few months after receiving permission to call itself the Old Vic Company.

During rehearsals for the tour of *A Murder is Announced*, I had the enormous excitement and pleasure of being awarded *The Times Educational Supplement* Senior Information Award for *Butterflies on my Mind*. Few accolades have given me more satisfaction. During the last week of the tour, I was offered the part of Delia in Alan Ayckbourn's *Bedroom Farce*. A perfect end to a very interesting year.

27

I don't know what I imagined Peter Hall would be like. Abrasive perhaps, and perhaps secretive. Overtly he is neither. He has a gentle manner, a beguiling sense of humour, magnetism, a very quick mind, and he is easy to work with. Unfortunately I had never taken over before, and I was anything but self-confident, which was a waste of time. If I couldn't trust myself, I should have trusted Peter, he had after all chosen me to play the part, but I was haunted by how Joan Hickson, a lovely actress, must have played it, and that isn't a creative way to think. Eventually I enormously enjoyed playing Delia. She is a disastrously funny woman and very truly written, but it took me a long time to live her truthfully, instead of playing safe with my idea of her and 'acting' her. Michael Aldridge, who had taken over the part of the pilchard-eating husband from Michael Gough, was extraordinarily kind and helpful, and wonderfully good in his part, and the play, like all Ayckbourn plays, is both beautifully observed, brilliantly comedic and fundamentally sad. I'm very glad I had the chance of trying her.

The show went extremely well. Originally it had been at the National, and was now in the West End at the Prince of Wales. Joan Hickson was playing it on Broadway. I was told I would be in it for three months. In the end I was there for eight or nine, and my Michael took over when Michael Aldridge had to leave to do some television. Michael actually opened in the part on the fortieth anniversary to the day of our first joint appearance in Aberdeen. Forty years on we were still together, both domestically and theatrically. I don't think in our wildest dreams, especially with war looming in 1939, we had thought we could possibly be so lucky. All those years later, I could remember a walk we had taken across Richmond Park on the day we had decided to become officially engaged, and on which we had discussed our future if we failed as actors. We had planned to go to America, with Michael as a butler and me as a lady's maid. Instead, here we were acting for the National, and still happiest in each other's company.

We had a very successful Ruby Wedding party with forty good

friends. Sadly two of our most beloved – Rebecca West and Jack Priestley – although both came, were not on speaking terms. We never found out why. But they found other congenial friends, luckily, and everything else went with a swing.

It was at about this time that our agent, Ronnie Waters, arranged a meeting with a television producer called Gerard Glaister, and it proved fruitful for each of us. Gerry has had a phenomenal run of success with the series he has set up and produced, including *The Brothers, Secret Army* and *Colditz*. He booked Michael for a part in the excellent series *Blood Money* straight away and later he cast him for much else. Luckily for me, he also dreamed up *Howards' Way*, and I have had six years of it.

In 1980, Michael was given one of his favourite parts on television, Wobbly Massingham in Molly Keane's *Good Behaviour*, and I had a tiny but astonishingly well-received part as a desiccated and sad old vendeuse in *Life After Death*. We also had a very happy engagement with Robert Eddison in William Douglas Home's play, *The Kingfisher*, at Windsor.

We saw Ralph Richardson while we were rehearsing for this, and he asked us what we were doing. We told him, and he said in that extraordinary mannered voice of his (smiling his own special smile of a schoolboy bursting with an amusement he oughtn't to be showing, while repressing the knowledge of an inner and wildly improbable secret), 'Ah yes. Gossamer on a tightrope.' He had played the part of Sir Cecil Warburton (the part Michael was to play) as he played every part I saw him in, to perfection; always strangely, while appearing to be very ordinary, and always with a vivid sub-text which illuminated the character in an unexpected way.

Edith Evans was once asked if she always understood everything she was saying in Shakespeare. 'Not always,' she confessed.

'Then what do you do?' she was asked.

She gave the questioner a sharp rather irritated look and said, 'I face front and I think dirty.'

Most of the really good actors not only live their parts, but make a sort of comment on them, and the comment is part of the fascination of the performances. I much regret I didn't see this particular comment of Edith's in action.

In 1981 we went on our first tour for Derek Nimmo in *Relatively Speaking*. Derek is an extraordinary man. (Michael later much enjoyed playing with him in *See How They Run* at the Shaftesbury.) He plays silly ass parts and is amusing and gentle in real life, as well as immensely clever and shrewd, but he runs his 'empire' of exotic touring dates in a splendidly managerial fashion, and the lucky actors involved in his plays stay in the best hotels all over the world, with board and lodging, laundry and cleaning all free. It is the life of Riley and tremendous fun.

Lucy Fleming, Simon Williams, Michael and I played in *Relatively Speaking* in Singapore, Hong Kong, Kuala Lumpur, Dubai, Abu Dhabi, Muscat and Bahrain.

Lucy had just been through a terrible tragedy. Her husband and little daughter had been drowned off a houseboat on the Thames. Simon's son and daughter, and Lucy's two little boys, all joined us in Hong Kong, and I think the enormous change from her life in England helped her a little to come to terms with what had happened. I hope so.

The sets for Derek's productions are each created in the place where the play is performed. They are made to measure so exactly that it feels as though the same set is being travelled for the whole tour. The plays are acted in the ballrooms of these great hotels, and the audiences arrive for a slap-up dinner, after which they stay on and see the play and have drinks in the interval. The idea is brilliant and extremely successful. The actors get their half-hour calls in their bedrooms, then make up, and get to the backstage area through the hotel kitchen.

For me, working out East was enormously satisfactory. I am almost always aware of my Malay origins and still love the country I then knew. Its beauty still obsesses my imagination, but Malaysia is now changing so fast that soon my memories will have no counterpart in reality. Singapore is no longer a tropical island of three races each sustained by their own national culture, but a rich, clean, spectacularly well-ordered Chinese shopping centre. Malaysia itself is becoming part of the new surge of fundamentalist Islam, while yet depending on Western tourism. Kuala Lumpur, that ravishing country town, is being despoiled by high-rise monstrosities, and the jungles are being invaded and destroyed. There is now a new resort not far from Kuala Lumpur which gives 'concrete jungle' a new meaning. Hong Kong, a miracle of capitalist success, is much uglier than it was, more overcrowded and, not unnaturally, frightened of the future.

In 1982, I had my own engagement in Chichester. It was an interesting play by Keith Baxter called *Cavell*, starring Joan Plowright

Dulcie Gray

as Nurse Edith Cavell, the Great War heroine shot as a spy by the Germans. I played her mother. I loved the job and Joan couldn't have been kinder or more co-operative to work with, but I found playing such a small part very frightening. In a large part, if you haven't done a scene to your liking, there are plenty more chances to put things right. In a small part, I almost felt as if I were doing a music hall turn and had far too much time to get nervous in the dressing-room. But Chichester has a very special atmosphere and public, and I would like to return one day – small or large part!

I saw Larry for the last time at Chichester. He had been constantly very ill, and that evening he looked it, until he began talking excitedly about his next job – a television production of *Lear*. He then became animated and well, and the years dropped away.

I published my first straight novel in 1982. *The Glanville Women* was highly praised by Rebecca who compared me to Thackeray, and the *Mail On Sunday* likened me to Arnold Bennett. Both reviews gave me pleasure!

The Glanville Women, a story of three generations of a theatrical family, is set in England and Malaya between 1910 and 1981. All three are looking for fulfilment and, like most women, they are deeply influenced by the men they meet, who threaten their independence. Most independent women have to meet this problem. Some solve it. Rebecca herself would have understood it only too well. Like the butterfly book, it had been in my head for several years and my move to Michael Joseph made it possible to write and publish it.

In 1982 we had the great privilege of entertaining Her Majesty Queen Elizabeth the Queen Mother to lunch. We had local friends to drinks first, then sat down at table ten strong. Her Majesty took the head and we sat Frankie Howerd at the other end with, between them, Lord Annaly (whose mother had been Her Majesty's Lady-in-Waiting when she was Duchess of York), Rebecca West, Dick and Mary Francis, and Anthony and Georgina Andrews.

Her Majesty was extraordinarily easy to entertain. Indeed she and Frankie made a wonderful double act which entertained *us*. Then after lunch she asked for Rebecca to sit by her. As she left, the caretaker and his wife and children, the local builder and his wife, and the game-keeper and his wife from the surrounding estate were presented to her in the hall.

On meeting the game-keeper she said, 'Mr Butters? Butters? Are you a friend of our game-keeper in Norfolk?'

[173]

Of course he was, and delighted that she had remembered. He died later that year and Mrs Butters told me that meeting the Queen Mother had been the peak moment of his life. Her Majesty has a magic – I have no precise idea wherein it lies, but it is a plain fact that everyone who met her that day felt actually happy and more alive, and Rebecca wrote to say that she had felt ill and old when she arrived, and well and euphoric by the time she left. What a gift.

The Queen Mother came again in 1985. John Gielgud escorted her, Michael Hordern with whom Michael had just been working, Lady Soames, Lady Daubeny, widow of Peter who had put on *The Wind is Ninety*, Lord Rawlinson, the son of Michael's charming Colonel in the war, and Christopher Cazenove and his lovely wife Angharad were our other guests. The second lunch party too was a wonderful occasion for us. Perhaps Her Majesty has such a cathartic effect because in some way she gives back to those to whom she talks a sense of their intrinsic value – an image of themselves as they would like to be – clever, witty, outgoing and good-tempered.

The years 1982–3 were full of work for both of us. I acted with Michael, first as an octogenarian murder victim in Ronald Millar's *Coat of Varnish* at the lovely Haymarket Theatre (London's most beautiful); to which we returned very successfully with Donald Sinden and Beryl Reid at the beginning of 1983 in *The School for Scandal*, Michael playing Sir Oliver and I Lady Sneerwell. We did a tour of *A Song at Twilight* – Noël's last play and one of his best. We played brothel keepers in *Rumpole* for John Mortimer on television, a documentary on Life in the English Country House, shot at Stansted (scene of my first public performance in 1938), and a radio play called *Are You Still Awake?* which we actually recorded lying on mattresses at Broadcasting House. We were also both given the honour of becoming CBEs – and had a lovely morning at Buckingham Palace. We were each allowed two guests – so we took Peter Donald, our first joint employer, and his wife Cleone, and Robert Lennard who had given Michael his first film break after the war, and his wife Kay.

We did a second season of *School for Scandal* the following year, this time at the Duke of York's, prior to a major European tour for the British Council. Beryl Reid couldn't do the tour, and Googie Withers was asked to take her place. Googie wasn't too keen on the part of Mrs Candour, so I took that over, and Googie played Lady Sneerwell. In our last week in London, I played Lady Sneerwell on one Saturday evening, and Mrs Candour (who talks quite a lot to

Lady Sneerwell) on the next Monday! We played sixteen cities in nine countries in ten weeks, and everywhere from Athens to Oslo it was spring. It was one of my favourite jobs ever. Googie is an almost perfect tour companion. She is a splendid actress, a beautiful woman, and endlessly kind and thoughtful. She rang me up almost every morning to ask if I would like to spend the day with her and her adorable husband, John McCallum, who had taken over from Michael. It was a joy to be with them. Everywhere we went, they found something interesting to see or do, and seeing Europe through their very intelligent eyes was indeed a bonus.

In Oslo, there was another of those strange little incidents that have so oddly peppered my life. Googie and I were reading the English papers in the lounge of the hotel on the day of the first night at the State Theatre, and found an obituary for our mutual friend, Peter Bull.

Some years before, Peter, Michael, Irene Handl and I had all been at a literary lunch in Stratford-on-Avon, plugging our books. Suddenly Peter had said, 'Do you believe in the after-life, Dulcie?'

'I don't know,' I said. 'Sometimes.'

'I do,' he replied, 'and you should. Indeed you must.'

'Belief is belief,' I said. 'Either you have it or you don't – or perhaps like me, you waver, but you can't make yourself believe.'

'You must believe,' he reiterated earnestly. 'I tell you what, when I die, I'll haunt you and then you'll have to believe.'

I made some non-committal reply and there, for the moment, the matter ended.

I told this story to Googie and we both laughed affectionately. She and John and I went across to the theatre about an hour and a half before the performance, and Googie came with me to see if my dressing-room was all right.

Peter, as anyone who knew him will remember, was mad on teddy bears. He kept a collection, and 'Aloysius', his favourite, was loaned out for the television of *Brideshead Revisited*. He wrote about teddy bears and even started a society for them. We talked about this on the way over.

We reached my dressing-room, I unlocked the door and threw it open. There was nothing at all in the room apart from the ordinary theatrical furnishings of a decent dressing-room, except – on the divan sat a positively enormous teddy bear! Googie went white and ran to her dressing-room, feeling quite ill with shock. I felt just the same.

The really weird thing was that no-one seemed to know where the bear had come from, or to where it had vanished when we returned for the show the following day.

A few months later, Michael and I did another Nimmo tour which this time included Thailand, Indonesia and Papua New Guinea. The play was a straightforward farce called *Here Comes the Bride* which also starred Derek Fowlds and Jenny Linden. In it was an excellent actor who won our admiration for the way he worked on his part at every performance, testing out the laughs, discarding the poor ones and keeping in the good ones. All actors do this of course up to a point, but Tony Anholt worked so well that an indifferent part legitimately became a very good one in a few weeks. When we reached Abu Dhabi he said, 'Dulcie, I've been offered a part in a television series called *Howards' Way*.'

'What a coincidence!' I exclaimed. 'I'm going to be in that.'

'I know,' he said. 'I shall be going into it after we leave Thailand.'

'I have to leave after Papua New Guinea,' I said.

So we joined each other for the first of the series in the spring.

In Jakarta in the hotel garden, in the enormous swimming pool, a tiny baby swam the length of the pool every day with its coach. Its mother – a failed Olympic swimmer – watched it. I hope it didn't strain its heart. It worried me terribly. But a plus was that the countryside was beautiful and the hotel had a wonderful scarlet and gold ceiling in the foyer. In Papua New Guinea, we unexpectedly played in the State Theatre. Port Moresby, the capital, is totally sophisticated and the hotel comfortable, but we went up into the mountains by air to a tiny place where Papuans who, fifty years ago had never seen a white man, let alone a car or an aeroplane, waited for us so that they could exchange places and do their shopping. In the magnificent Parliament building at Port Moresby, a debate was going on when we visited it, between a Government Minister in black jacket worn over a sarong and speaking with an impeccable Oxford accent, and a member of the opposition speaking in pidgin, interspersed frequently with the word bugger, which is used more or less as we use the word trouble. Christ is called, quite reverently, 'Him buggered-up on the Cross'.

Instead of flying home direct from Papua, I went with the others to Hong Kong. It was just as well because Joy Shelton, who came out to take over from me, completely lost her voice, and I was able to stay and play until she was fit.

ctogenarian murder victim in Ronald Millar's *A Coat of Varnish* at the Theatre Royal, Haymarket.

Above: A delightful lunch party. Standing from the left, Michael, Frankie Howerd, Lord Annaly, An[
Andrews, Dick Francis; (seated) Rebecca West, HM Queen Elizabeth the Queen Mother, Dulcie, Georgina And

Below: In *The Best of Friends* as Dame Laurentia McLachlan with Michael and Frank Thornton.

In 1986 I did nine months of *Howards' Way*, then *See How They Run* with Michael at Windsor. In 1987, I was again in *Howards' Way* for nine months and then *The Living Room* at the Royalty Theatre in London, where I met Graham Greene again, whom I hadn't seen since *Brighton Rock* in 1943. He wrote a charming letter from Antibes and as I love his work it was a delight to know I had pleased him.

In 1988 and 1989, I also did *Howards' Way*. It took up quite a large part of the year as usual – i.e. February until the end of October. In 1990 only until September – perhaps a BBC saving? The rehearsals took place at Acton in what is laughingly known as the Actors' Hilton where nearly all the BBC dramas are rehearsed. The canteen food is pretty drab but it's a good place for meeting friends. The interior recordings were done every ten days or so, for two or three days, at Pebble Mill in Birmingham, and the exterior filming was done at various places round Southampton, or on locations abroad such as Malta, Guernsey and Bermuda. We had BBC designers to buy our clothes for the show (which after series five we could buy back at sixty per cent of their original price after the series was over), and it was a happy steady job.

We became a sort of family, and the death of Maurice Colbourne hit us all badly. He was an exceptionally nice man, mad about horse-racing and fishing, and it is sad that he died so young, before he could enjoy the fruits of success. He'd had an impecunious childhood in Sheffield, and had only begun to make good as an actor shortly before he came into *Howards' Way*.

The public were very faithful to the series and the average audience was ten million. For us as entertainers, this was obviously good news. Each year it was lovely to see each other again. I learnt to enjoy clothes (never a priority with me although, during the 'fifties and 'sixties, I had clothes from Dior, Rahvis and Hartnell), and always working with people younger than I am kept me in touch with the present. Strangely enough, although clothes have never been important to me in 'real life', as an actress I depend on them enormously. Until I have 'seen' my character made up and dressed, I am not absolutely sure who she is. Once I know how she looks, I know how she feels and behaves.

1989 was our Golden Wedding year. We began by acting in *The Chalk Garden* at Windsor with a wonderful cast, Helena Bonham Carter, Eleanor Bron and David Swift. Unfortunately, we had a good deal of extramural publicity to do and I also had to do a day's work on a television play, so I didn't have enough rehearsal time for such an intricate, mannered and difficult part as Mrs St Maugham and, on the opening night, I dried twice.

Every actor forgets his lines some time in his life, but I have always had the facility to make up appropriate ones until I am back on beam again. This time I couldn't, and it really threw me. For the next few days, I suffered from stage fright and no illness I have ever had has worried me more. Life became a nightmare. From the moment I woke up, I was sweating with fright. Usually, although I'm nervous at every performance and terrified on first nights, I am not aware of what I call the 'shadow of the evening' – which is the sort of nervous internal preparation I make for each evening performance – until about four o'clock.

In the dressing-room, my throat dried up and my tongue seemed to have thickened. On stage I said everything in my head before I said it aloud, instead of listening to my fellow actors. It was monstrous. Then one day the fright disappeared as completely as it came, and things were back to normal. A horrible experience.

The play was a complete sell-out, for the whole time we were there. To our great excitement, Queen Elizabeth the Queen Mother brought the Queen and Duke of Edinburgh to a performance and asked us back to Royal Lodge for supper afterwards. It was a wonderful evening.

I had taken seven episodes of *Howards' Way* off to be with Michael. We did a couple of touring dates with *The Chalk Garden*, then some television together.

We were 're-married' on April 29th at St Saviour's, Walton Street, where we had first agreed to stay together 'in sickness and in health'. The church was filled with friendly actors and Michael Hordern read the lesson beautifully. We had a reception at the Lansdowne Club, where Robert Flemyng made a very touching speech and, later, we gave two large parties at home in the country. The Gallery First Nighters gave us a dinner, as did the Green Room and the Savage Club, and Frankie Howerd made a very funny speech at the first of these. Frankie is one of the three best speech-makers I have met. (The others are the first Lord Birkett and Ned Sherrin.) He manages to give the same impression of unscripted hilarity that he does while performing; indeed his speeches are a kind of very personal extension of his performances. His long rather charming face with its thatched hair and brisk eyebrows, becomes a little manic, and his mouth becomes the moue of an aggressive baby. He produces in his audiences a feeling of enormous affection. We now look forward to our Diamond Wedding.

28

East is East and West is West nor ever the twain shall meet, Kipling opined with confidence. But he got it all wrong as far as I am concerned. My life has spanned East and West and the twain are still meeting. My lost paradise is not my childhood but the jungle at Fraser's Hill. The three countries of my mind's eye are Malaysia, England and the theatre, and both as actress and writer I travel them still.

It has been an interesting and rewarding life. Materially it has brought everything we wanted, creatively I should have liked some times to have been more stretched. But we have been blessed with marvellous friends, on and off stage, and have kept in work. Statistics are sometimes surprising. Looking back through our engagement books over the years, I find I have to date done 106 plays (over forty in the West End) and twenty films (starring in eight), plus hundreds of radio broadcasts (395 in *Front Line Family* alone), and what can best be described as numerous television shows. Michael has done more plays than I but fewer films and broadcasts. He was on the Equity Council for twenty-seven years, and Vice-President three times. We have had the good fortune to work hard in the profession we love.

As a writer, my other profession, this is my twenty-fourth published book; there have also been two plays, six broadcast radio plays adapted from my books, many short horror stories, and short stories and articles in many magazines and newspapers. I am a compulsive writer and feel empty and itchy if I'm not writing something. I'm often asked why I work so hard. I like to, and perhaps boarding school at three and a half set an unconscious pattern.

Now we are old, I am not afraid of death. Why should I be? No-one has returned to say that the other life is really hell, but I am afraid of the manner of dying. I dread the thought of dependence, incontinence, blindness, deafness, paralysis and strokes. Old age is not for weaklings or for the queasy either. Just as we are too young when we are young

[180]

to realise what a gift from the gods youth is, we're really too old when we're old to undergo the trials of old age! Like marriage, they come to us without proper training. Still, survival is what all nature is striving for and, so far, we have survived.

I am not reconciled to old age yet. I've had little to grumble at so far, but aesthetically I dislike my physical dilapidations. Other people's attitude to old age is also depressing. Many of the young find the effort to communicate too much, others are too reverent. The young are also frightened of a glimpse into their own future, so real old age disgusts them. I'm afraid I shan't grow old gracefully, but warily and critically. On the other hand, there is no denying that it is a passionately interesting time. And if new little hazards manifest themselves yearly, so do new small luxuries. Lovely not to be shy any more, and lovely to be more concerned whether I like my companions than whether they like me. I have the satisfaction of being a self-made woman, and many of my particular pleasures intensify – watching butterflies, walking among wild flowers, browsing in antique shops, looking at pictures, reading books, and naturally, going to the theatre.

Memories don't dim – or haven't yet.

Dogs have played a large part in our lives. Bonnie, our first corgi, made five films and two trailers at Elstree, and loved every minute he was acting. The two labradors who spent the next thirty years of our lives with us – Titus who lived for sixteen years and Prospero, who lived for fourteen – were not natural actors. Titus was in a play, and never made a mistake, but Michael's dresser had to take him to the pub next door after he had done his piece, where he had arrow-root biscuits to calm his nerves.

Our present dog Brett, a beautifully marked tri-colour corgi, came to us rather late, at eight months, from the kennels where he was to become a stud dog. He took to his new home with great enthusiasm, and to guarding it with rather too much relish. He also barked all through telephone calls which made it almost impossible to hold a conversation. We told this to Katie Boyle who sent us a tape she had made with John Fisher, a dog psychologist, on dog training. We went to see John Fisher with our problem, and in his office Brett immediately took up position close by the door. Mr Fisher told Michael that if Brett were going to benefit from the hour's session, he would, at some time during the interview, leave the door, and come and sit close beside Michael instead. Twenty minutes later Brett did exactly that. Apparently Brett had thought he was an alpha dog – the leader of the pack – as he hadn't been trained early to living with humans and he had to be shown that Michael was the alpha figure. We were given some advice, and a strange little collection of brass discs on a scarlet ribbon, and told that if we did what Mr Fisher had suggested all would be well. We were also told not to smack him or beat him, which relieved us.

When we reached home Brett sat on the rug in front of the fire, deep in thought. The result was magic. He was transformed, and now even steps aside to let me go through doors first!

The last time someone fell in love with me I was sixty. Since then it has been downhill all the way! The smoke signals of desire used to be fun, and in a life which hasn't exactly been a rake's progress of sex, its intimations have been exhilarating. Yet how amazing sex is, and how important that we live through the debris of our most urgent early desires to come to know ourselves so that we can become adult.

The future of the planet bothers me, as it does most other people! Victorian clergymen pursued butterflies whose beauty intensified their belief in God. However, they caught and killed them and impaled them on setting boards. Humans are the cruellest creatures on earth. We are nature's pollutants. My favourite book is *The Parable of the Beast* by John N. Bleibtreu. His description of the life cycle of the cattle tick is for me totally riveting. The Dean of Trinity Hall, Cambridge, the Rev. John Polkinghome, is quoted as saying, 'There is a quality about the best ideas which is self-authenticating. The fact that the world is shot through with so much that is mathematically beautiful is, in a sense, the physical evidence of the working of a Mind.' Right on the nose for me.

As a child I was told that all diseases were caused by the tiny red and white corpuscles in our bodies, fighting, and I came to the conclusion that humans might be corpuscles in an enormous being which incorporates the sun, moon and stars, and that its mind was God. I still have a misty feeling that there is something in that idea.

A sense of awe went out with the eclipse of candlelight, and its passing has diminished our feeling of kinship with nature, and our need, acknowledged or not, of a faith by which to steer ourselves. I believe that art, poetry and architecture, not to mention our development as human beings, have all suffered in this spiritual vacuum. For forty years, too, I have had a vivid sense that we are, in reality, watching a film of our lives, past, present and to come. Whether or not what we are watching can be edited or changed, I don't know.

I love actors as a species. They are larger than life and can be egotistical, I know, but so can businessmen, politicians, clergymen and greengrocers. At least most actors are generous and entertaining, and if when they are together they talk about their work, why shouldn't they? Other people do. In all my career I have only detested five actors. Not bad in fifty years.

What about our future in the theatre? Michael's and mine, I mean. Like most actors we don't know. Last year I did thirteen episodes of *Howards' Way*, five recitals (one at Windsor Castle), three broadcasts and a national tour. But this year? Next year? The year after? Neither Michael nor I have any wish to retire. As long as I can see and think rationally, I shall write.

That fate should have nudged a plain, rather lost but determined little girl from Kuala Lumpur in the direction it did, has been surprising but much appreciated. The terror of losing my memory and not working again, which is the fear of all actors, the passionate excitement of reading a good play or seeing the first butterfly in the spring, the hope of writing a good book, and the joy of Michael's company, are still with me. And I find that stimulating.

After the magnificent service for Laurence Olivier in Westminster Abbey, someone said to us, 'Wonderful, of course, but a bit much, don't you think? After all, he was only an actor.'

Only an actor indeed!

Dubedat in Shaw's *The Doctor's Dilemma* says, 'I believe in Michaelangelo, Velazquez and Rembrandt; in the might of design, the mystery of colour, the redemption of all things by beauty everlasting, and the message of Art . . . ' He is talking about painting, but great acting, great music and great writing all signal their fanfare of glory, too.

For myself, however, I will settle happily for 'only an actress'.

A PROFESSIONAL CHRONOLOGY

Key: F, Film; L, London; M, Musical; O, Overseas; P, Play; R, Radio;
T, Tour; TV, Television

1938 First public performance:
Maria in *School for Scandal*
(Lord Bessborough's private
theatre, Stansted Park)

First performance with MD,
as Kitty O'Shea and Parnell
in *Parnell* at the Webber
Douglas.

1939 In Aberdeen
Plays include:

Hay Fever	P
On Approval	P
Love From a Stranger	P
Outward Bound	P
Dear Brutus	P
The Young Idea	P
Night Must Fall (for the troops)	TP

1940 H.M. Tennent Company
(Edinburgh & Glasgow)
Plays include:

Music at Night	P
The Silver Cord	P
Spring Meeting	P
Last of Mrs Cheyney	P

White Rose Players
(Harrogate)
Plays include:

The Importance of Being Earnest	P
The Shining Hour	P
Ma's Bit of Brass	P
The Middle Watch	P

1941 *Front Line Family* (395 broadcasts) — R

1942 First London performances
(Open Air Theatre,
Regent's Park):

Twelfth Night (Maria)	LP
'The Shrew' (Bianca)	LP
'The Dream' (Hermia)	LP
The Little Foxes	LP

1943

Brighton Rock	T & LP
Landslide	T & LP
2000 Women	F
Madonna of the Seven Moons	F

1944

A Place of One's Own	F
They Were Sisters	F
Lady From Edinburgh	
(i) OT to liberated Europe	
(ii) Tour in UK	
(iii) LP	

1945

Wanted for Murder	F
The Years Between	F

[185]

1946	*Dear Ruth*	LP
	The Wind is Ninety	LP
	Signed up by Korda.	
	Fools Rush In	TP
	A Man About the House	F
	Mine Own Executioner	F
1947	*My Brother Jonathan*	F
	With MD co-starring	
1948	*The Glass Mountain*	F
	Rain on the Just	T & LP
	(first joint West End	
	appearance with MD)	
1949	*The Will*	TV
	Queen Elizabeth Slept	
	Here	T & LP
	Crime Passionelle	TV
1950	*Queen Elizabeth Slept*	
	Here	T & LP
	The Franchise Affair	TV
	The Fourposter	T & LP
1951	*Angels One Five*	F
	Milestones	TV
	See You Later (Revue)	L
1952	*Dragon's Mouth*	T & LP
	There Was a Young Lady	F
	Sweet Peril	T & LP
1953	*Art and Opportunity*	TV
	A Fish in the Family	TV
	The Distant Hill	TP
1954	*Diary of a Nobody*	LP
	We Must Kill Toni	T & LP
	Olympia	TV
	Fourposter and *Private*	
	Lives	OTP
	(South Africa)	

1955	*September Revue*	TV
	Alice Through the Looking	
	Glass	LMP
1956	*The Sun Divorce*	TV
	Love Affair	T & LP
	(Author and actress)	
	Lesson in Love	TV
	South Sea Bubble	OP
	(South Africa)	
	Tea and Sympathy	OP
	(Australia)	
1957	*South Sea Bubble*	OP
	(return to South Africa)	
	The Governess	TV
	2 Episodes of *Boyd Q.C.*	TV
1958	*Double Cross*	LP
	Take Copernicus	TMP
	(author, but didn't act in it,	
	renamed *Love à la Carte*)	
	Epitaph for George Dillon	TP
	Double Cross	TP
	The Importance of Being	
	Earnest	TV
	Candida (Oxford)	P
1959	*Let Them Eat Cake*	T & LP
	The Best Cellar	TP
1960	*Candida* (London)	T & LP
	Winter Cruise	TV
	Murder on the Stairs	R
	The Letter	TV
1961	*The Bald Prima Donna*	TP
	Candida	TP
	The Chairs	TP
	Heartbreak House	T & LP
1962	*Village Wooing*	OTV & OP
	A Marriage Has Been	
	Arranged	OP

Shakespeare Recital
(Berlin) OP
Royal Gambit TP
Virtue TV

1963 *Where Angels Fear to*
    Tread T & LP

1964 *Where Angels Fear to*
    Tread L & TP
    (continues)
    Merely Players OTP & TP
    (Shakespeare recital)
    The Seagull
    (Birmingham) TP

1965 *Beautiful For Ever* TV
    A Man Could Get Killed F
    An Ideal Husband T & LP

1966 *Ideal Husband* LP
    (continues)
    On Approval T & LP
    We Beg to Differ R

1967 *On Approval* L & TP
    Happy Family LP
    No. 10 T, OT, LP

1968 *Vacant Possession* TP
    Confessions at Night TP
    (Nottingham)
    Out of the Question T & LP

1969 *Out of the Question* LP
    (continues)
    Trio: *The Will*
        Village Wooing TPs
        Ways & Means
    Unexpectedly Vacant TV

1970 *How He Lied to Her*
    Husband LP

Village Wooing LP
Press Cuttings LP
Dandy Dick TP
Wild Duck T & LP

1971 *Clandestine Marriage* TP
    School for Scandal TP
    Village Wooing TP
    Unexpectedly Vacant TP

1972 *Dragon Variation* TP
    (Windsor)
    Alice Through the Looking
        Glass TP
    Hay Fever TP
    Ghosts TP

1973 *Dragon Variation* TP
    At the End of the
        Day T & LP
    This is Your Life TV

1974 *At the End of the Day* LP
    (continues)
    The Sack Race T & LP
    The Pay Off T & LP

1975 *The Pay Off* (continues) LP
    Time and the Conways TP

1976 *Carry On Jeeves* TP
    Ladies in Retirement TP
    Façade (Recital with
    orchestra at the Queen
    Elizabeth Hall, London, and
    at Nottingham)
    Time and the Conways TP

1977 *The Cabinet Minister* TP
    (M's adaptation of Pinero)
    A Murder is
        Announced T & LP

1978	*A Murder is*	
	Announced	LP & T
	(continues)	
	Bedroom Farce	LP
	(for National Theatre)	
	Voysey Inheritance	TV

| 1979 | *Bedroom Farce* | LP |
| | (continues) | |

1980	*The Kingfisher* (Windsor)	TP
	The Cherry Orchard	TP
	(Exeter)	
	Lloyd George Knew My	
	Father	TP

1981	*Relatively Speaking*	OTP
	(Far and Middle Eastern	
	tour for Derek Nimmo)	
	The Kingfisher	TP
	Life After Death	TV

1982	*Pink Panther*	F
	Agatha Christie	TV
	Coat of Varnish	LP
	Cavell	TP
	(Chichester)	
	School for Scandal	TP

1983	*School for Scandal*	LP
	Tartuffe	TP
	A Song at Twilight	TP
	Rumpole	TV
	The Thirties (Stansted)	TV
	Are You Still Awake?	R

1984	*School for Scandal*	LP
	(as Lady Sneerwell)	
	School for Scandal	LP, OTP
	(as Mrs Candour)	
	One episode of *Cold*	
	Warrior	TV

1985	*There Goes the Bride*	OTP
	(Far and Middle Eastern	
	tour for Derek Nimmo)	
	Howards' Way	TV
	(1st series)	
	Lloyd George Knew My	
	Father	R

1986	*Howards' Way*	TV
	(2nd series)	
	Mrs Donaldson at Sixty	R
	On Approval	R
	See How They Run	P
	(Windsor)	

1987	*Howards' Way*	TV
	(3rd series)	
	The Living Room	LP

1988	*Howards' Way*	TV
	(4th series)	
	A Song at Twilight	R
	A Visit to Remember	TV
	(Interview with Brian	
	Johnston)	
	Three Up Two Down	TV
	An Evening with the	
	Denisons	
	(Recital at Claydon)	

1989	*Howards' Way*	TV
	(5th series)	
	The Chalk Garden	TP
	Three Up Two Down	TV
	An Evening with the	
	Denisons	
	(Recital in Manchester	
	Square, London)	
	A Visit to Remember	TV
	(1 hour)	
	Myself When Young	R
	A Festival of Poetry	
	(Recital in Cheltenham)	

What's My Line?	TV	
The Hit Man	R	
An Evening with the Denisons		
(Recital in Manchester)		
Gardening Quiz	R	
Edward Seago Programme	TV	
The French Revolution		
(Recitals at Stratford)		
Relative Values		
(A reading at Sonning)	P	

1990	*Howards' Way*	TV
	(6th series)	
	An Evening with the Denisons	
	(Recitals at Sheffield,	
	Blackpool, Chipping	
	Norton, Ludlow)	

Shakespeare Recital for Sam
Wanamaker
(RSA award, at Windsor
Castle)
'Vienna' with the Cornel
Group
(Concert at Dorchester and
Harrow)

What's My Line?		TV
Gala Concert for Queen		
Elizabeth the Queen		
Mother's Ninetieth		
Birthday		
(Palladium)		
Three episodes of *Mrs*		
Donaldson at Sixty		R
The Best of Friends		TP

INDEX

A complete list of plays and films is contained in the Professional Chronology on pp 185–9

[191]

Dulcie Gray

Salberg, Derek 125
Salew, John D. 141–2
Saunders, Peter 147, 168
Schofield, Paul 162
School for Scandal 160, 174–5
Seago, Edward 152, 189
Selangor Club (Spotted Dog) 12, 35
Shaw, George Bernard 16, 53, 61, 143, 157
Shaw, Glen Byam 59, 121, 146, 157–8
Shakespeare, William 54, 61, 76, 121, 125, 143, 147, 171, 187, 189
Sheffield, Lyceum Theatre 139
Shelton, Joy 176
Sherek, Henry 100, 125–6, 129
Shine, Bill 115
Shingler, Helen 60
Sickert, Walter 112
Sim, Alistair 152
Simpson, Mrs Wallis 46–7
Sinden, Donald 174
Sitwell, Edith 163–4
Sitwell, Sacheverell 163
Sleep, Wayne 160
Smith, C. Aubrey 97
Smith, Maggie 158
Soames, Lady 174
Society of Authors 127
Society of West End Theatre Managers 141
Somerset, Anne 55, 60, 69
South Africa 120, 126, 128–9, 132, 186
Spencer, Gladys 74
Spenser, Jeremy 140
Stansted 60–1, 65, 174, 185, 188
Stiebel, Victor 150
Stevenson, Margot 116–17
Stratford-upon-Avon 121, 123, 125, 146, 175, 189
Sultans of Malaya 26, 29, 36, 51
Sumatra 42
Sutro, John 107
Swift, David 177
Symons, Julian 132, 138

Tafler, Sydney 115
Take Copernicus 112, 118, 136

Tandy, Jessica 107
Taylor, Elizabeth 106
Tempest, Marie 57, 73
Tennant, H. M. 69–71, 185
Terraine, Molly 58
Terry, Ellen 57
Terry, Phyllis Neilson 137
Terry-Thomas 92
Tey, Josephine 106
Teynac, Maurice 119
Theatre of Comedy Company 157
They Were Sisters 86–7, 90, 92
Thorburn, Carina 53
Thorndyke, Sybil 155
Thorne, Angela 14
Todd, Richard 148
Tonks, Henry 11
Travers, Ben 84
Tredgold, Dr 118, 151
Trewin, J. C. 125
Tutin, Dorothy 111
Twelfth Night 76–7
Tynan, Kenneth 111, 113–14, 121–2, 127, 150

Uncle Jum (Godfather) 21, 42, 64
Uruguay Film Festival 107

Van Thal, Herbert 128, 143, 151, 166
Venice Film Festival 108–9
Vivian, Lord 127

Wallach, Ira 154
Walton, William 164
Warner, David 155
Watergate (Theatre) 110
Waters, Ronnie 171
Webb, Beatrice 16
Webb, Sydney 16
Webber Douglas Drama School 53–4, 59, 61, 63, 78, 110, 149, 185
Weldon, Duncan 160–1, 165, 168
Welles, Orson 108–9, 122
Wells, H. G. 163
West, Rebecca 138, 162–3, 171, 173–4
Whatmore's, A. R. (Wattie) London Players 63, 65, 67, 69–70